AGE OF NEW POSSIBILITIES

ALSO BY REINHARD MOHN

Success Through Partnership:
An Entrepreneurial Strategy

Humanity Wins

AN AGE OF NEW POSSIBILITIES

How Humane Values and an Entrepreneurial Spirit Will Lead Us into the Future

REINHARD MOHN

CROWN PUBLISHERS
NEW YORK

Published by Crown Publishers, New York, New York.
Member of the Crown Publishing Group, a division of Random House, Inc.
www.crownpublishing.com

CROWN is a trademark and the Crown colophon is a registered trademark of Random House, Inc.

Printed in the United States of America

Design by Lauren Dong

Library of Congress Cataloging-in-Publication Data
Mohn, Reinhard
    [Gesellschaftliche Verantwortung des Unternehmers. English]
    An age of new possibilities : how humane values and an entrepreneurial spirit will lead us into the future / Reinhard Mohn.—1st ed.
        p. cm.
    1. Social responsibility of business. 2. Entrepreneurship—Social aspects.
3. Quality of work life. 4. Corporate culture. 5. Industries—Social aspects.
6. Public-private sector cooperation. 7. Industrial sociology. I. Title.
HD60 .M6413 2004
174—dc22   2004012393

ISBN 1-4000-5344-7

10 9 8 7 6 5 4 3 2 1

First Edition

I gratefully dedicate this book to the many helpful people in our company who have stood by my side as I developed Bertelsmann's enterprise culture, offering encouragement, counsel, and constructive criticism. I owe this gratitude most particularly to my wife!

CONTENTS

FOREWORD

Both as an entrepreneur and as a Foundation member, Reinhard Mohn does all he can in deed as well as word to further the cause of justice, welfare, progress, and peaceful coexistence among the peoples of this world.

With this book he offers politicians and public administrators the benefit of his rich fund of experience gained from more than fifty years of dynamic and creative involvement in the private sector. Using concrete examples, he explores the ways in which successful initiatives in the business world can be carried over into the public sector to bring about necessary reforms. Reinhard Mohn offers interesting recommendations for reform in a variety of areas such as motivation of the workforce, delegation, and subsidiarity. Particularly in a period when people are increasingly weary of politics, these suggestions ought to prove especially interesting to those in positions of responsibility in politics and public service.

Reinhard Mohn is a severe-looking man—scarcely surprising in someone who has borne heavy responsibility over many years. But in conversation it soon becomes clear beyond all doubt that his heart belongs to humanity and humane values. Dialogue, commitment, solidarity, ethical convictions, as well as efficiency, are the essential elements in his vision of a better and more sustainable future for the world and for each and every local community.

We, his friends, colleagues, and readers in the Club of Rome, are delighted and grateful that Reinhard Mohn, one of our Honorary Members and Governor of our Club of Rome Foundation, is publishing this impressive book full of his forceful convictions and insights, all of them based on his solid experience of life.

—*Ricardo Diez Hochleitner,*
Honorary President of the Club of Rome

Eberhard von Koerber,
Vice-President of the Club of Rome

I

NEW PREMISES FOR THE GOALS AND
METHODS OF THE ENTREPRENEUR

INTRODUCTION

In the course of my professional career as an entrepreneur I have come to know a great variety of social and economic systems. Both the successes and the failures that I have encountered in the process have made me aware that, given the dramatically different conditions that now affect people's lives, it is high time to develop new goals and new approaches. Any future order of things, however, can endure only if it is in accord with humane principles and, above all, with the very different way in which people now perceive themselves.

If we are to develop new aims and objectives for the future, there is relatively little to be gained by looking back at the past. In our present circumstances it is more a question of using our creativity, our powers of judgment, our ability to give shape to things, in order to discover a new and appropriate path. It seems to me that the entrepreneur has the best qualifications for this task. For in order to succeed, entrepreneurs have always been compelled to adapt to people's wishes and to respond rapidly to change. The competitive world of the market economy tolerates neither dogmatic systems nor forms of behavior that run counter to the essential nature of mankind. To give one example of the very different circumstances in which we now live: In earlier days, it was obligatory within the context of the state to preserve traditions and stick rigidly to rules and regulations. Since progress in the sense of steady change did not yet figure among society's aims, the sole criterion for judging the work of public servants was its "orderliness." In our present age of global competition between different systems, however, this "orderliness"—in other words, this dogged adherence to outdated habits—would be a dangerous error.

THE MARKET

Since time immemorial, the production of goods and services has been organized on the basis of the division of labor. The interchange of supply and demand used to take place in the "marketplace," or at any rate via the "market," this exchange process being made considerably easier through the introduction of money.

Supply increased in scale and range as a result of the development of science and technology, while the market expanded due to burgeoning competition and the growth of advertising. Then improvements in communications and transportation allowed the once purely regional market to broaden into the global market of today.

Politicians, however, were relatively slow to grasp the importance of the market for people's standard of living and their general sense of contentment, and for this reason it was long believed that national sovereignty could also be extended to include the economy. Today, however, all the most important national markets have open borders. They have opened themselves up to a free and global exchange of goods.

OUR CULTURE IN A STATE OF FLUX

The good old days in which almost everything followed a well-established pattern have long gone. Today, differences of opinion regarding aims and methods lead to serious arguments and bitter disputes on a global rather than a merely regional scale. The body of shared values that a society must have in order to remain a coherent community is in tatters. International cooperation is bedevilled by egotism, dogma, and the thirst for power, factors which have not infrequently resulted in chaos marked by conflict, severe hardship, and misery, and have even led to the collapse of the relevant country's political structures. Those in positions of responsibility must therefore come to realize that the premises and rules enabling people to live together in a truly humane way and to enjoy a stable social order have fundamentally changed!

Already in the twentieth century change was taking place with unprecedented speed. But it will become even faster due to the increase in knowledge and its ready availability! Whereas people in earlier ages developed their culture on the basis of traditions that all had experienced, we in our current process of change have not managed to bring the various international social orders into harmony with one another. In earlier periods of civilization, social systems were directly determined by the ruling elite with their own particular experiences and their determination as the key influences, and they sought to achieve their ends by instituting hierarchical structures. Even value systems, so indispensable to the life of any community, were laid down by those in power entirely at their own discretion! So long as such systems were able to prevail, those in power had no incentive to change. On the contrary, since change of any kind always appeared to harbor risks as well as possible benefits, what mattered was to strive to maintain the status quo— especially by fostering tradition. To those in power this manner of organizing society seemed most likely to guarantee a lasting and secure state of affairs. As to what might be in the best interests of their subjects: they never gave it a thought.

In China, for instance, this kind of rule continued for very long periods of time. However, it presupposed that any external or internal impetus for change could be resisted—something that was largely achievable in China thanks to its geographical situation. For the nation's subjects at that time, issues such as "dissatisfaction with their standard of living" or "the demand for progress" simply didn't exist.

In Europe, on the other hand, the dominant groups in culture and politics did not always manage to achieve a comparable degree of durability. Indeed it was a particular feature of European countries that they found themselves caught up in an ever accelerating process of political, economic, and social change, and had to try to survive in the face of constant threats and great instability. Repeated attempts to ensure continuity by establishing dynasties and imposing sociopolitical dogmas of one kind or another increasingly failed because of the inadequate leadership skills produced by such systems.

AN AGE OF NEW POSSIBILITIES

Today, technical progress and the general increase in knowledge allow people to aspire to a better standard of living and to demand more freedom to shape their own lives in the way they wish. The question of how to realize these goals, however, is the subject of constant and heated discussion on all sides—though these controversies are frequently characterized by self-interested political maneuvering on the part of the various social groups, who thus display a lack of objectivity and fairness. But let us console ourselves with the fact that it always takes time to fashion a new culture— and this applies equally to the current state of development of our own democracy and to the process of modernizing Germany's economic system!

In the meantime, the bad experiences of the past few decades— and also their successes—have taught us that quality of leadership is the key determinant of success in all areas of life. It is no doubt regrettable that this knowledge has not yet made sufficient impact on the way our current systems are evolving, but we should nonetheless take care not to be premature in seeking to enshrine new social and political systems in law, for we in Europe are currently in a very good position to see just how problematic dogmatism and inflexibility really are.

What we do need now, on the other hand, is full acceptance of the European Union, and the ability to develop effective management methodologies that make it possible to delegate responsibility downward, and to spark new impulses from these lower echelons. In trying to bring this about, we need to bear in mind that the top echelons in the various organizations making up our society lack the requisite competence, and are therefore hopelessly overstretched and incapable of succeeding in their task. The impetus for reform is therefore very unlikely to come from this quarter. Our reflections on these matters may well receive considerable stimulus from the example of progressive large companies, from the example of democracy and the political involvement implicit in its form of civil society!

BRINGING MANAGEMENT METHODOLOGY UP-TO-DATE

In undertaking this task of developing a new management methodology we must not let ourselves be seduced into paying undue attention to regional or group-specific interests and hence producing solutions that are not designed first and foremost to benefit the majority. Since in Germany, too, sheer size and power still play a dangerously large role, those who run the various organizations within our society must abandon their dogged adherence to established hierarchical positions. This is a path that leads nowhere, and the failure that it would unquestionably result in could well prove disastrous. Monopolies are not a good thing either in the economy or in society as a whole!

The impetus for accomplishing the necessary reforms will probably not come from the realms of politics or academia, nor will it come from those now in power. It will come instead from people who excel in independent thought, creativity, and community spirit. To put this another way: It might well be that by developing a decentralized civil society we shall arrive at the kind of management methodology that we need in order to have leaders and managers in politics and the public service who are genuinely suited to their functions and are capable of learning new things.

The learning process will presumably happen more quickly in the private sector, since greater pressure is exerted here by the realities of competition. Businesses with outdated hierarchies or wrong goals—an exclusive focus on maximizing profit, for example—cannot unlock the flexibility, commitment, and creativity in people that today's circumstances demand. Speaking generally, we can say that large concerns—and I include the apparatus of the state here—will have a much more difficult time handling these reforms than medium-size businesses will, since in large state organizations any form of management involving creativity and enterprise is for the most part deliberately reined in to minimize risk, and to ensure that all staff achieve similar levels of performance.

Attempts at the political level to balance the different interests within society, and the antagonistic discussions between the representatives of the various groups involved, have considerable consequences for the economy given the very diverse conditions under which it has to work—but scarcely any attention is paid to these consequences. The politically attractive goal of "equality" is inappropriate to the economic realm in terms of both issues and people. The government dreamed up the idea of "round table" discussions—on the labor market and the health system, for instance—but this initiative, too, has largely failed to impress. After all, it doesn't begin to tackle the real causes of the ever more apparent mess in which we find ourselves, for those involved think that with the backing of the country's political leadership they can push the "right" solution through, without regard to the very different objectives involved or the necessary financial room for maneuver. People will soon have to realize, however, that even when it comes to the general good, there are limits to what is possible. It should already be giving us pause that the figures both for productivity growth in the German economy and for Germany's gross national product are looking increasingly poor in comparison with the rest of Europe!

It is perhaps only by looking at the practice in other countries that we will come to realize that the many interventions on the part of government on the one hand and employer/union negotiating bodies on the other do not improve workers' pay, benefits, or living conditions in the public or private sector, but in reality worsen them. And perhaps we will also realize that entrepreneurial management and the performance-orientation principle still represent the best available management methodology—and one that is gravely damaged by constant state interventions! We should also recognize that the "culture of conflict" that is considered such a laudable feature of a parliamentary democracy constitutes a seriously disruptive factor within the economic sphere with its success-oriented objectives. In today's businesses with their necessarily highly decentralized structures, the worst thing one can do is to undermine the motivation of the workforce, as this makes it impossible to operate a decentralized, entrepreneurial management system—a system based on motivation, creativity, and commitment, and the only one capable of handling a task that will become ever more difficult as time goes on. What we need are people willing to commit themselves to their particular company with all their creative talent—and we need this kind of commitment at every management level. We must accordingly strive to maximize people's motivation, and we must see to it that they identify with the goals of their organization. But if we practice a culture of conflict in the private sector then we achieve exactly the opposite effect!

Adversarialism has its place within a democracy. But management of any enterprise that is performance-driven and subject to competition needs a workforce willing to cooperate and to identify with the organization and its aims. What it does *not* need is a culture of conflict! So far as the public sector is concerned, it would almost seem as if we had learned nothing from the failure of the centralized planned economies in the socialist countries. Even the countries of the Third World have meanwhile shown a better understanding of the implications: they are putting their faith in competition, individual initiative, decentralization, and entrepreneurial creativity. We, too, should say good-bye to old habits of mind. Though it is true that to do this we need detailed knowledge of the relevant field, sincerity, and the courage to implement reforms!

2

NEW GOALS FOR THE STATE, NEW GOALS FOR THE ECONOMY

THE PATH TO NEW GOALS

The original aim of the economy, namely to meet the population's needs in respect to goods and services, remains the same as it ever was. And the same applies, so it seems, to the aims and incentives of capital. For, as in the past and doubtless also in the future as well, those who possess capital today seek to increase their wealth. In respect to the function of capital within the context of a business, however, decisive changes have occurred. The widespread but fallacious view that capital plays the leading role here is a hangover from the period when great fortunes were being amassed, a period when the realities of industrialization meant that particularly enterprising ventures led to the accumulation of vast amounts of capital. As most people at that time had no clear understanding of the multifarious functions of an entrepreneur, they characterized entrepreneurs quite simply in terms of their most conspicuous feature, namely their "wealth," and defined them as

AN AGE OF NEW POSSIBILITIES   25

"suppliers of capital." This designation was indeed apt in respect to the original entrepreneur, the introduction of corporations resulted in a distinct separation of the functions of management on the one hand, and supply of capital on the other. The ensuing battles over the division of responsibilities gave rise to the rather imprecise distinction between "capital" and "labor." But we should not lose sight of the fact that in reality the most important success factor in any business is its *management*! An accurate characterization of the various groups involved would therefore need to distinguish between "management," "capital," and "labor"—though in most cases today the influence of management is far greater than the impact of investors in the form of "financing" and "boardroom oversight." Particularly in difficult economic situations everything depends first and foremost on the skill of the management!

This state of affairs is well illustrated by the socially very significant problem of ensuring continuity when ownership passes from one generation to the next. For not every inheritor is capable of fulfilling the role of entrepreneur, and attempts to do so often result in the company's demise. We must therefore draw a distinction between the shaping role of the entrepreneur and the function of capital as now generally practiced. The contribution of capital as, among other things, an overall control mechanism does indeed remain extremely significant—but it is the entrepreneur with his entrepreneurial flair who shapes the company's progress.

The increasing dependency of employees on the management style of their companies has led, over the course of the last century, to serious protests and interventions on the part of both the unions and the state, but none of this has produced a method of bringing influence to bear that is fully appropriate to the situation or compatible with the needs of the economy. The employers bemoan the increasing restrictions on the scope of their decision making and the financial burdens imposed on them; the unions demand more solidarity and a bigger say; when things develop in the wrong direction politicians attempt in their own particular way to remedy the situation by trying out corrective measures—as in the case of nonwage labor costs—that say very little for their business skills, as the example of the labor market clearly demonstrates. In these days of modern communications it would be easy to draw comparisons with other countries as regards the principles behind government financing. But the politicians responsible do not appear to be interested in this. In order to retain power they wish to prove that their way is the correct one! Here we really do have to speak of a flaw in the system—all the more so given the fact that in this country political competition very clearly doesn't entail enough in the way of sanctions.

Faced by stagnation in the economy, the public is slowly realizing that the many interventions by government and by the various parties involved in wage negotiations do not improve the performance of either the state or the economy, but in reality hinder it! The state, its politicians, and the unions all need to grasp the fact that entrepreneurial management of an organization still represents the best available management methodology. If today this form of management can be given modern expression through the enterprise culture system, then all involved will achieve the degree of engagement and identification with their organization that will enable us to withstand global competition and once again reach a top position in the international rankings. Furthermore, within the context of a true enterprise culture a due sense of involvement on the part of a company's stakeholders can be achieved much more easily and effectively than is the case if one is sitting around a table with the putative assistance of politicians.

THE CONSEQUENCES OF A NEW
CONCEPTION OF MAN

It is not only the market and the conditions of production that have changed over the course of the previous two centuries but also people's whole perceptions of themselves. The improvement in the standard of living and the increase in educational opportunities have reinforced people's desire for freedom and control over their own lives. The traditional and plainly inadequate attempts at reform on the part of the old autocracy and the appalling conditions arising from the capitalist economy of the period repeatedly posed the question as to how a more humane and more just society could be brought about. However, the resulting attempts to work out solutions to this problem only served to confirm the evidence of history that the creation of new social systems entails a gestation period lasting hundreds of years.

In our own era, too, people aspire to a higher standard of living, a greater degree of social justice, and the opportunity to try their luck as best they can. Given the stagnation prevailing on all sides and the many things seriously wrong with the way the country is run, people are no longer willing to be quieted by promises. They want to share in any progress, and they want results! The aspiration to "orderliness" is a thing of the past, for it no longer accords with what is necessary and possible. Our citizens expect reforms that allow them to take part in public life and to acquire real influence and responsibility. These aspirations are indeed inherent in the concepts of democracy and a market economy, but as yet they have been realized only to a quite limited degree. For instead of pursuing decentralization and deregulation, the political and economic powers-that-be are still seeking to justify themselves by pointing to past successes. They have clearly not even begun to understand the new possibilities that are available, and they also fear that reforms might result in their losing power! Relevant proposals for change, which often emanate from those with the least say, therefore tend to be suppressed on the grounds that they threaten the proper order of things. Could it by any chance be the case that in the twentieth century too, as so often before, erstwhile revolutionaries turned into jealous guardians of the status quo?

In what follows we shall address ourselves to problems that are overdue for consideration and in urgent need of a solution. We must necessarily start by taking a hard look at our social goals and our current ways of running things. Are these goals still in accord with people's expectations, and does their implementation exploit all the possibilities now afforded by modern management techniques and methods?

Many German citizens today expect more from the state than the services it customarily provides. Influenced by politicians who believe that the state can accomplish all things, they have become accustomed to seeing a steady improvement in their standard of living and a constant expansion in state benefits—accompanied by a reduction in the fiscal burden on individuals. The claim for government assistance, originally put forward on the principle of "solidarity," has now reached the point where people can enjoy a tolerable standard of living without even having to do much work in the underground economy—whereas the concept of "subsidiarity," of self-help, and of taking responsibility for one's own life has all but disappeared from our vocabulary.* The consequences of this wrong conception of society may be seen at present, in Germany, in the state's empty tills, the stagnation of the gross national product, and ever-increasing unemployment.

Now this situation is not something ordained by Fate, but is attributable to a clear failure on the part of the country's political leadership! A democracy must indeed concern itself with the welfare of its citizens, but not in a way that renders it incapable of taking appropriate action!

The form of democracy practiced in the United States offers us a particularly apt example of an alternative political concept. "As little state as possible": that is the firm conviction of Americans. But in exchange, the citizens of America are quite prepared to do whatever is in their power to order public affairs both well and, above all, in the way that best suits them. This form of democracy, known as a "civil society," is more flexible and more efficient. The citizens' level of satisfaction is established by means of frequent opinion polls, and appropriate steps are taken in light of the results. The provision of services is allocated on a competitive basis, and is open to private companies. This entirely different concept of democracy means that, while taxes are much lower, social prosperity and economic productivity can grow at a much faster rate. It is no wonder that U.S. citizens are proud of their democracy, which they themselves have largely shaped, whereas German citizens tend to feel

---

* Translator's note: "Subsidiarity" is essentially a sociopolitical concept relating to the overall fabric of society and the respective roles of government and citizenry. The supplement to the *Oxford English Dictionary* defines it as "the principle that a central authority should have a subsidiary function, performing only those tasks which cannot be performed effectively at a more immediate or local level"; note also the quotation dated 1976: "According to the doctrine of subsidiarity . . . social problems should be dealt with at the most immediate (or local) level consistent with their solution."

despair at the intolerable features to be found at every turn in their own state.

To summarize the implications of this discussion, we can see that there is a pressing need for Germany, too, to change its understanding of democracy. You simply can't get democracy for nothing! Our political leadership must demand a truly democratic demeanor on the part of its citizens, and must ensure that it is brought into being. All German citizens, including the unemployed and those in need of assistance, must take on their full share of responsibility and make the fullest contribution of which they are capable! By relearning the principles of a civil society we shall attain a better and "leaner" democracy that would be a successful alternative to our present practice of making undeliverable election promises and vilifying our political opponents. In any event, I am quite certain that a new democratic style of this sort can be brought about in our country, too, and would be appreciated by the voters!

The same applies in the economic sphere. The modes of work now prevalent in our economy require that the traditional, hierarchical mode of management be relinquished, for best performance in terms of quantity, quality, cost, and flexibility can only be achieved through a decentralized form of organization that relies on the motivation and commitment of its employees. Having been brought up to value their independence, people today no longer wish simply to receive orders. Rather, they are fully prepared to take responsibility and to make their own personal contribution to the success of the enterprise. We should therefore make every effort to dismantle the traditional hierarchical structures that still prevail in this country and instead take the American example of a civil society as our model. In my own experience I have repeatedly found that this is not only possible but also far more successful! For the knowledge that they have made a personal contribution to the success of the enterprise gives our colleagues at all levels a much greater sense of satisfaction (just as happens with citizens in a civil society) and enables them to see a real point to their work.

LEADERSHIP AND ITS LEGITIMATION

The legitimation of power by means of a constitution played a very different role in the earlier history of mankind from the one familiar to us in the democracies of today. In earlier epochs the acquisition of power was generally the result of military conquest. Those who gained a monopoly of power tended to create laws designed to legitimize and consolidate the power gained through force of arms and, almost invariably, to the advantage of their immediate or wider families—a process that one can still observe in numerous Third World countries today. It is certainly true that these largely dynastic succession arrangements prevented a power vacuum, and also ensured that over long periods of time the successive heirs could claim to be qualified for their task. But the flaw in the system lay in the privileging of a particular group, who thus had the potential to exploit their power in an uncontrolled and predominantly self-interested fashion. Many efforts were made to prevent such unfortunate developments but were ultimately incapable of excluding the risk of someone inheriting power who was insufficiently qualified for the role of leader, and hence also of excluding the consequences that inept leadership brings with it.

If we are offering a critique of political systems, however, it is only fair to point out that our own democratic system is not entirely proof against the danger of groups being formed for the purpose of abusing power. There are many examples that bear this out. The proponents of democracy retort that a government that nobody wants can be voted out of office at any time, but unfortunately this argument is dangerously tenuous in an age when the media have supreme influence. In our country, however, the power of other social groups rests less and less on traditional power positions and instead depends increasingly on their proficiency and their ability to keep demonstrating this proficiency. This is particularly clear in the economic realm, where firms have to hold their own in a free market with all its competitive pressures, and thus justify their existence. This market-economy system combines a socially desirable power-control mechanism and an irresistible obligation to be both proficient and progressive. The fact that the continuance of this state of affairs is guaranteed through the law's prohibition of cartels further serves to strengthen this system.

But whereas in the case of a market economy we may take it that the system as a whole proves its credentials by virtue of its continuing success, this does not necessarily hold true for an individual company, for the economic development of entire industries as well as individual companies depends not only on the market and on their workforce, but also on other influential factors such as capital, unions, and state intervention. These factors are not similarly subject to competition, they do not possess the same flexibility, and they respond very inadequately to market forces!

Here, too, however, modern management techniques offer at least a partial solution to the increasingly difficult problems involved in management. I refer to the following possibilities:

1. More delegation of responsibility to lower levels, and a correspondingly organized planning and management information system.
2. The specializing of functions and the harmonizing of procedures by means of coordinating committees that ease the burden on higher management levels.
3. Central direction of the planning and management information system.
4. Forward-looking and long-term development with respect to management personnel needs.
5. Motivation of staff through clear definition of the company's enterprise culture, and exemplary conduct on the part of management.

EVERY MANAGER MUST BE MONITORED BY SOMEONE HIGHER IN THE ORGANIZATION

In view of the now indispensable need for the delegation of responsibility, these rules have become an even more important aspect of management methodology. Management personnel in particular must therefore identify with the goals of the company and set aside their personal interests, since excessive ambition and personal vanity in a manager can lead to serious problems. Wrong attitudes of this kind must be prevented by the inclusion of relevant provisions in a company Code of Conduct.

Fortunately, these days there are also possibilities within the *non*economic sphere for making people's efficiency and their personal suitability for a given task measurable and therefore assessable, although these methods for enhancing efficiency and assessing staff have so far been little appreciated or put into effect. A large potential reservoir of productive energy and creativity lies waiting here that could, in particular, be usefully deployed within politics and the public service, in the context both of the job "on the ground" and of personnel work. The market has shown us highly suitable ways of accomplishing this. The relevant processes are known as "performance orientation" and "competition."

These criteria should be applied above all in the evaluation of managerial staff, since management is the key success factor in all spheres of activity. It is the job of management to concretize goals and to see to it that all the various people involved are fully focused on the goal of their group. In these days of decentralized responsibility, management must take particular pains to ensure that the distinct but disparate interests of all the groups involved are attuned to the times and taken fully into account. Continuity and sustained success can be achieved in a time of change only by dealing with things in ways that are fully suited both to the task itself and to the people performing it! To ensure that those who lead have a legitimate claim to their positions, we must modernize our personnel work, re-examine our goals, and establish new yardsticks!

The public is gradually becoming aware of these issues, although the various thoughts that have been aired with respect to a redistribution of power have not yet led to any generally accepted set of solutions. Inflexible systems like the hierarchically organized public service, dogma-based systems such as we see in a "planned economy," and the various forms of common ownership have all shown themselves thus far to be neither functionally appropriate nor sufficiently adaptable. Even that form of capitalist society that is standard practice in our economy today and—at least within certain limits—functionally effective, still has to make strenuous efforts in order to overcome its built-in failings and maintain the legitimacy of its way of running things. What people most readily accept are ways of running things that are performance driven and lead to competitive outcomes. Given that for most people criteria such as fairness, self-fulfillment, and solidarity are especially important, compromise solutions are necessary for the time being—and also feasible. Attempts to find partial solutions—such as profit sharing in the private sector—are therefore quite right for society within the context of such developments, and in the longer term clearly offer a way forward.

Nevertheless, this present phase of development in which new management methodologies are being put to the test will need to continue for a long time yet, since the shortcomings that we have criticized cannot be remedied by decree, but only through a careful learning process. But this doesn't mean that one has to behave as in the old days and meekly accept whatever appalling things the powers-that-be inflict on us. On the contrary: Through a steady succession of reforms we must move ever closer to an optimal management system in all areas of life, even though in a period of change this demands from all of us much honest endeavor and a willingness to experiment!

ACCEPTING AND DEALING WITH CHANGE

In times of change many of our mental habits need to be challenged. This applies both to the actual definition of our goals and values, and to the ways in which we seek to achieve them. In view of the very different circumstances in which we now live we have to be prepared to embrace reforms, while at the same time bearing in mind that cultural change must not be implemented in ways that overstretch people's capacity to learn. This means that alongside our support of reforms we must also show patience and an ability to evaluate proposed changes with respect to their effectiveness and long-term consequences. These problems are clearly exemplified in the current debate within the European Union concerning the integration of immigrants from diverse ethnic backgrounds. The difficulties that this involves in terms of adaptation are likely to require our attention for quite a few decades.

Amid all these far-reaching processes of change it must remain a matter of considerable importance to us to preserve a certain degree of continuity and to avoid at all costs trying to solve problems by force of arms, for military might is no way to fashion progress. It is not war that is the father of all things, as Heraclitus thought, but peaceful competition between different systems—and thanks to the ease of making global comparisons it is always possible today to cast around for better solutions in almost every sphere of life.

However, a worldwide competition between all the various systems would entail the danger of the weak being driven to the wall by the strong. Thus the competitiveness of our own society must not be our only concern; we must also be careful to ensure that global differences in development do not become unbridgeably large! In the political realm there is a growing awareness that poverty and despair can breed dangerous instability. To deal effectively with change and to ensure social continuity, therefore, we must make every effort to see to it that the reform process takes place in a constructive manner and on a global scale. This demands a very high degree of learning ability, and will be correspondingly burdensome! But there is no serious alternative. We can therefore summarize the position as follows: Our political goals should be determined in such a way that they enable us to play a full part in the march of progress, while at the same time bolstering the continuity that is inherent in peaceful global development.

3

THE NEW MANAGEMENT PHILOSOPHY
IN THE ECONOMY

THE ENTREPRENEURIAL MODE OF MANAGEMENT

In my experience an entrepreneurial approach to economic processes supported by the rights of control conferred by ownership is the optimal form of management when a business is first being formed, for entrepreneurial management brings with it the right and the freedom to shape the business in the most appropriate way, together with a share in any profits or losses, all of which greatly aids the learning process. This process adds a necessary extra dimension to the entrepreneur's theoretical training, and given our present state of knowledge could scarcely be improved upon—in terms of society as well as in the business sense.

It is possible to re-create almost all these entrepreneurial conditions, even in large companies. The first step is to choose management trainees who combine personal integrity with creativity, courage, good judgment, and a sound understanding of human nature. The working conditions of management trainees in a profit center should allow them real freedom, and should be geared to the principle of "learning by doing." However, the prerequisite for a successful career in any company dedicated to enterprise culture is a complete willingness on the trainee's part to accept the goals and values of the company and to set them above any personal aspirations they may have in other directions!

After a relatively short familiarization period in the company the trainee should be given a task involving independent action in a smallish profit center. A goal should be set for this task that is clearly measurable in extent and profitability; in addition, it is particularly important to observe how well the trainee is accepted by the staff on a purely human level. As soon as the profit center's figures show positive results stemming directly from the trainee's management initiatives, he can be put on a profit-sharing scheme, though this must not be allowed to restrict the company's freedom to deploy the trainee as it sees fit.

Young trainees must learn at an early stage what an impact their own personal behavior has on the willingness of staff to give of their best. The authority of managers and their mandate within the company should be grounded in a combination of skill and an exemplary attitude. The personal goals and management style of an aspiring manager must focus primarily on the success of the company, and must not run counter to the rules and regulations in force within the company as a whole. Annual surveys of staff opinion must include questions that check whether a manager has indeed observed these rules and regulations. The conduct of each manager must be assessed in a special meeting with their line manager, and corrective action taken if necessary.

Large companies today must realize that their performance, and indeed their continued existence, can no longer be allowed to depend chiefly on the discipline of a hierarchical organization; instead, every effort must be made to ensure that management and staff identify with their company's goals. Discipline is undoubtedly necessary as well—but to command the future, identification with the company is more important. Today it is this attitude alone that makes it possible to delegate responsibility to lower levels—a practice essential for effective management, and one that companies will scarcely be able to avoid in future if they wish to remain competitive! Here we can also see a major reason why "return on capital" is not acceptable these days as a company's sole aim. It is in these terms, then, that enterprise culture and its new goals must be made to prevail.

FAIR PAY FOR MANAGERIAL STAFF

In our present day and age the task of management is becoming ever more difficult. Competition has become ever more severe and can completely alter a company's market position within an extremely short space of time. The increasing size of companies also presents management with additional challenges!

The result of these changed circumstances is a rise in the number of bankruptcies on the one hand and, on the other, a growing need for better managers—a need that has led over the past few years to such immense pay increases for top managers that the public has been provoked to great indignation, and not entirely without reason! For when a company is close to collapse and the workforce have to accept a reduction in their pay, it is indeed difficult to understand why an employee at the top of the company should receive bonuses running into millions. This has just recently provoked renewed criticism of the capitalist system, and I therefore think it appropriate to offer a few comments at this point:

1. Capitalism has spread across the whole world not because it is fair, but because it constitutes the most efficient economic system yet known. It results in a better standard of living for the population of any country that adopts it. Compared to this advantage, its systemic *dis*advantages appear bearable and indeed not infrequently remediable.

2. An entrepreneur's performance finds graphic expression in his balance sheet. A comparison with competing companies in the same sector makes this balance sheet even more eloquent. It should be noted in passing, however, that the remuneration of a salaried manager and the profit of an entrepreneur can be compared only to a very limited extent given that each has a different function—as soon becomes clear if we consider the example of entrepreneurial risk.

3. As the working atmosphere exerts a marked influence on a company's efficiency, it would be a good idea if "social balance sheets" were better conceived and more widely used!

4. The problem of fair pay for management staff cannot be solved by a generally applicable pay scale. It is not the nature of the particular job that chiefly determines the level of remuneration, but the extent to which the job is successfully accomplished! In other words, it is proven success that constitutes the key criterion where a manager is concerned. This can be put into effect if a considerable proportion of an individual's remuneration is determined afresh each year in line with the degree of success actually

achieved. In this context, however, we also need to bear in mind that it is becoming increasingly difficult to find suitable candidates for senior management positions. Just as with goods and services, the "market" in managers reacts to an inadequate supply by raising its prices. But this is not of fundamental importance to our economy's ability to function, as the increased efforts by both the education system and the private sector to provide more training will make good the current deficit in the medium term. For all its flaws, however, our present economic system is still far superior to any state-managed economy. We only have to look at the world market to see the rightness of this assertion!

5. As this book is chiefly concerned with bringing our economic system up-to-date, I should like in this context of "fair pay" to refer once again to the new enterprise culture that is now emerging:

- With regard to pay, the management concept implicit in the enterprise culture system requires that there be "fairness for all *in accordance with their performance*"!
- As regards "fair pay," profit sharing is recommended for the workforce as a whole!
- The pay of managerial staff should be determined according to each individual's level of success; it should fall within the normal range of salaries prevailing in the private sector; and it should show performance-related differentials.

Let us close this section by quoting Article 14 of Germany's Basic Law, which declares that "ownership carries obligations." If we take this principle fully to heart in our approach to enterprise culture, then in my view we have done what is truly necessary.

ENSURING LEADERSHIP CAPABILITY

With regard to ensuring adequate leadership capability, it becomes particularly clear in cases where a company passes to an heir how problematic it is that ownership automatically confers rights of control. So long as it remained relatively easy to run an economic enterprise—as used to be the case in agriculture and the craft trades, for instance—the "family business" perfectly exemplified the concept of handing property down through successive generations over very long periods of time. However, the circumstances no longer exist that made it relatively easy to run a business! We now have a situation where in medium-size businesses the transfer of managerial control succeeds only in some 35 percent of cases. When it comes to the *third* generation the success rate falls to 10 percent—and in large companies it amounts to a mere 0.1 percent!

If the entrepreneur has the good fortune to find suitable successors among his children, then the process of preparing them for their eventual assumption of control should begin as early as possible. For no one learns how to run a business by suddenly waking up one day to find himself thrust into the hot seat, for although this avoids dissension between father and son, it spells great danger for the continuity of the enterprise; one learns how to run a business by acquiring thorough theoretical and practical experience. For this reason, too, it seems highly advisable for the children of an entrepreneur to spend a lengthy period of time abroad.

A potential successor's first managerial task—taking over responsibility for a profit center, for instance—must serve as a practical lesson in handling people correctly and in realizing profits. If this first step is successfully accomplished, consideration can also be given to awarding him a share of the profit center's profits.

In the course of his further training the child should, if at all possible, gain experience in *all* important aspects of the business, for instance, marketing, personnel, and intracompany information systems. This was the pattern I followed in offering my children the opportunity to try their luck in their own businesses. In the meantime, they have taken over responsibility for various parts of the Bertelsmann company, and although fathers do tend to overestimate their children's progress, I think I am justified in my expectation—based on others' judgment as well as my own—that some of them will in due course have considerable influence on the running of the company! This family contribution to securing continuity of leadership for Bertelsmann fills me with hope, delight, and reassurance all at the same time.

As an alternative to family succession, the business can either be sold to a competent entrepreneur, or someone not belonging to the family can be groomed to take over the reins. These standard solutions, too, need careful planning over a sufficient period of time. It is not uncommon these days, especially in the case of medium-size companies, to find that the arrangements for transferring control are put in place too late, and are not sorted out in an appropriate manner—with mostly dire consequences for all concerned. The task of securing continuity of leadership must accordingly be regarded within the context of medium-size businesses as a social as well as a private matter—and I would refer once again here to the article in the Basic Law declaring that "ownership carries obligations"! Clinging to possessions and power is, humanly speaking, very understandable—but it certainly does nothing to help maintain entrepreneurial activity in the economy. In the long run society will not accept a situation where the departure of an entrepreneur means the demise of his enterprise. We therefore can and must see to it that this particular drawback of entrepreneurial activity is mitigated—and it is astonishing that no political initiatives have yet been taken in this direction.

At Bertelsmann I have transferred most of the company's shares into a nonprofit-making foundation, thus perpetuating the attitudes and aspirations of my forebears. The statutes of this foundation provide for

- leadership by people with entrepreneurial talent;
- continuity of our corporate people-oriented constitution;
- aims and objectives that reflect humane values and serve to foster society's capacity for working together as a community.

Now that this business concept has been tried and tested over a period of many years, there are grounds for hoping that we have managed to develop a model that brings out the best in people, and that holds its own in competition with other economic systems. In particular, this model enables the great advantages of the entrepreneurial mode of management to be not merely retained but even enhanced. I believe that this kind of enterprise culture fulfills my obligation to society, and also that it represents a major advance in the methodology of management.

There is one other particular feature that I would like to stress with respect to cases where there is a failure to ensure continuity of leadership in an economic enterprise. The international economic crisis of 2002 led to the collapse of an extraordinarily large number of businesses. Along with inadequate financial arrangements, another factor that played its part with striking frequency was the sheer inadequacy of the people in charge due to their excessive vanity. In selecting potential managers I always used to pay careful attention to the character and personality of candidates as well as their professional qualifications; but in view of the downfall of so many managers at the present time, I have to confess that I didn't really give sufficient thought to the problem of vanity. This doubtless has to do with the fact that the men I earmarked for training as managers were still relatively young, and in the course of their learning process up to that point had scarcely had occasion to give a presentation of their achievements, so that it was not always easy to form a definitive judgment as to their personal qualities, which tend to become particularly evident when people deliver these formal presentations. And of course it is a vain disposition more than anything else that often shows itself only when the individual has achieved a certain degree of success. Those managers who are now coming unstuck on an international scale were clearly given too much scope to indulge their vanity and were insufficiently subject to corrective measures on the part of those to whom they were answerable. But once one has become accustomed to plaudits, one misses them all the more when energy slackens and successes are no longer so plentiful. The thirst for fame has driven many a manager to "heroic deeds" and caused him to make major, and irresponsible, investments.

The fact that this pattern becomes more marked in periods of economic crisis may explain the current remarkably high incidence of bad decisions. No tears would need to be shed about this if it were simply a matter of the manager in question losing his personal prestige, but such failures of leadership often bring disaster for thousands and cause the downfall of whole companies. There is thus an urgent need for action on this score.

With respect to securing continuity of leadership in large companies, the question is whether the consequences of excessive vanity can be identified and neutralized before it is too late. This question is a very tricky one, as companies are scarcely going to decide to replace the man at the top without very pressing reasons! I therefore cannot offer any universally valid solution to this problem. Nonetheless, I do recommend keeping a careful watch on the personal motivation of managers. For people betray their vanity by massaging their image to curry favor with the public, seeking maximum exposure in the press, and representing their company—or their own ego—at countless social functions. Politicians may well gain by behaving in this way, but for managers it is often merely a question of indulging their vanity, an activity for which they should really have no spare time.

Managers who incline to vanity very rarely encounter any correctives to their behavior within their own professional circle, which is why vanity—particularly in the top echelons of management—can lead to such disastrous consequences. It seems to me extremely doubtful whether any kind of well-intentioned advisory discussion—for instance on the topic of the individual's personal goals and aspirations—could bring about a change in this sort of temperament. Vain managers are egocentric and resistant to influence: They always think they know better!

DANGERS ON THE PATH TO POWER

Anyone aspiring to a position of power within the private sector needs to possess qualities that far exceed the norm in terms of resolve and proficiency. Professional expertise must be accompanied by a good understanding of human nature, exemplary personal behavior, good judgment, creative ability, and a capacity for self-criticism. Since any major project these days can only be carried through with the help of others, the man at the top must ensure that their goals, too, are geared to the interests and well-being of society as a whole. But anyone who has not learned to cope satisfactorily at the grass-roots level and, by so doing, achieve success in a profit-oriented management task, is going to have difficulties when faced with more important tasks, especially if he allows himself to be driven by vanity, egotism, and a thirst for power.

The top man in a company must not only have practical intelligence but must also conduct himself in such a way that he can serve as a model to the company's staff. To this end it is imperative that he accept the values and rules necessary for good social interaction within the company, and that he make them the basis of his own actions.

The sheer range and difficulty of the task of management today make delegation of responsibility an essential requirement. However, if a manager's personal demeanor makes it impossible for his staff to identify with him and his management style, then he is going to be incapable both of delegating and of leading successfully. Anyone in the world of work who does not regard his staff as his partners leaves himself no scope whatever to be effective. Instead of applying the efficient principle of delegation he has to exercise his leadership role by imposing his authority and by resorting to tight control and discipline—a far less effective regime. He will also have to forgo the advantage of being surrounded by motivated staff.

Since we know that negative temperaments in people can be changed only to a very limited extent, it is necessary to prevent temperamentally unreliable managers from advancing very far within a company. For where there is an increase in responsibility, accompanied in most cases by increased freedom of action, managers of this kind represent a major risk for the company, particularly if they allow themselves to be driven by an unhealthy desire for grandeur and praise. In this context one has to ask why continuous flawed behavior on the part of a manager does not get corrected in good time. Well, for one thing a manager's superiors still exercise very strict control over him during his early years on the job, and, for another, he doesn't yet have any individual successes to his credit. It is only when the manager has risen to a position where he has more freedom of action and is less subject to supervision that the dangers of vanity begin to wreak their effect and become more evident.

To take an example: A manager driven by vanity and personal ambition can achieve an astonishing increase in turnover within a relatively short period of time by buying up companies, and then at press conferences and other public events bask in the plaudits of his confreres. But it is precisely this kind of forced growth that dangerously overstretches a business's management and workforce. For the integration of newly acquired companies necessarily requires time and patience and involves heavy costs, and where there is sustained expansion of this kind it only takes a few years for the changes in profitability and liquidity to start causing concern when the annual accounts are presented. If the man at the top, bent on further enhancing his own image, also puts pressure on those within the organization to achieve even faster growth, then trouble and danger are just around the corner!

Managers pandering to their vanity lose little sleep over such growth problems; they can simply borrow or, where necessary, raise capital through the stock market. They remain unconcerned, too, by the problematic fact that by the very nature of their expansion strategy the newly acquired companies cannot possibly be satisfactorily integrated into the business as a whole, since they do not have the requisite funds or managerial staff. He considers such nuts-and-bolts tasks to be a second-order problem that other people can sort out.

It is true that this kind of strategy aimed at garnering public plaudits can dramatically increase turnover for a few years—but sooner or later the critical moment will come when liquidity is endangered and losses are realized. To prevent this, it is therefore necessary to get rid of egocentric managers at a sufficiently early stage to prevent further damage. This was the practice followed by Jack Welch at General Electric. Anyone in his company who delivered less than he had promised, for instance with respect to his budget, was given one more chance and then fired—on the grounds that a major company must be able to delegate and, in so doing, must be able to rely on its managers. The principle of delegation of responsibility is simply nullified in the case of overambitious opportunists who promise more than they can deliver—and for this reason they are, in Jack Welch's view, unfit to be managers in a major company!

The economy finds itself faced today with enormous new challenges, and the relevant learning processes are on a correspondingly large scale. The number of firms that have failed in these new circumstances has reached an unprecedented and worrying level that seems to throw into question the management skills of the entire economy. In many of the collapses of major companies that we see, huge amounts of capital and huge numbers of jobs are lost, and often it is the vanity of a manager that is solely to blame.

———※———

IT IS ALL the more important that in the future the Supervisory Board, as the responsible body in such matters, intervene in good time. The members of this body must show independence of mind, they must have the courage to act, and they must ensure that the interests of the company take precedence over the grand plans of a would-be big wheel who may often seem imaginative, but is in truth irresponsible!

EVALUATING THE LEADERSHIP POTENTIAL OF EXISTING STAFF WITH A VIEW TO THEIR SUCCEEDING TO POSITIONS ON THE EXECUTIVE BOARD

Ensuring continuity of personnel on the Board of Directors is the responsibility of the Chairman of the Board and the Personnel Committee of the Supervisory Board.* It is a task that requires long-term planning. Reports on relevant developments should be presented to the Personnel Committee every six months, and to the full Supervisory Board every twelve months!

To optimize this process it is necessary to take account of all available options, and thus to consider both internal candidates and candidates from the open market. For this purpose it is advisable to use the services of recruitment agencies. A preparatory period of at least two years should be allowed prior to the Executive Board making its decision. In the case of candidates from within

* Translator's note: German companies not only have a *Vorstand,* more or less equivalent to an Executive Board or Board of Directors, but also an *Aufsichtsrat.* As American and British companies don't have this particular hierarchy, there are no directly equivalent terms in English.

the company this period can be considerably shorter. Due attention must be made to assessments already in existence as a result of the routine staff assessment program.

When judging the merits of a candidate for appointment to the Executive Board, careful attention should be paid to the following:

I. Clear evidence that the candidate has proved proficient and successful in carrying out his management responsibilities, with particular reference to the following:

1. Previous management tasks, and the results achieved (see relevant management information system data).
2. Information from the candidate's line manager regarding his ability to work under pressure.
3. The candidate's own personal conception of his goals. It must be clearly established whether he identifies with the tenets and culture of the company.
4. In the case of internal applicants it is essential to have the results of staff opinion surveys available. In the case of external applicants a detailed assessment should be commissioned from a recruitment agency.
5. A major portion of the proposed annual pay package should be performance related. The remuneration level should be in line with prevailing norms for such posts.
6. The candidate's personal conduct must be exemplary, and must clearly display
   - leadership ability;
   - identification with the tenets of enterprise culture;
   - willingness to put the company's interests before his own;
   - honesty and reliability;

- commitment to the needs of society;
- openness to the international dimension.

Where shortcomings become apparent, it should be borne in mind that it is practically impossible to change negative characteristics for the better! If candidates are interviewed by the Supervisory Board they should be carefully questioned with respect to the above-mentioned positive characteristics.

II. Common sources of error in assessing candidates for executive positions

Companies have very limited experience with respect to making appointments to their Executive Boards. Numerous potential mistakes can therefore be avoided by making use of a suitably specialized recruitment agency. The search for appropriate candidates, and the process of forming an opinion on their merits, are thereby rendered objective, and gain in quality. This is especially the case when the post in question is international in scope.

Successful management requires both professional experience of the relevant field of activity and also the ability to lead and motivate people effectively. Out-and-out egocentrics are therefore of no use for leadership tasks, no matter what successes they may have to their credit in other respects. "Autocratic stars" are doomed to failure in any company with a marked enterprise culture. The following principles thus apply to management of a company at Executive Board level:

- Senior managers must identify with the enterprise culture system.
- The complexity of the task makes delegation imperative.

- It is an essential prerequisite that staff be motivated and that they identify with the company's goals.
- The management approach must be entrepreneurial, performance oriented, and based on a spirit of partnership.

A check must be made at least once a year to ensure that these requirements are being adhered to. To this end, full account should be taken of the evidence contained in the company's management information system, the results of staff opinion surveys, and assessments provided by the individual's two immediate superiors. The Supervisory Board's Personnel Committee must report orally and in writing to the full Board on the measures it is taking to ensure that the Executive Board remains at all times fully and effectively staffed.

If shortcomings repeatedly come to light in the way a potential member of the Executive Board carries out his managerial duties, then arrangements must be put in place to appoint someone else! Management staff are to be informed of this provision.

REASONS FOR DEVELOPING
A NEW ENTERPRISE CULTURE

Businesses emerged in the old days thanks to the initiative of entrepreneurially gifted individuals who, in the relatively straightforward conditions of the time, were able to use an authoritarian mode of management to achieve remarkable success. Based on the wealth acquired thereby, and aided by the rights of control conferred by ownership, larger, hierarchical enterprises then began to develop. There was no question here of considering the needs of individuals or of society as a whole, and hence no friction with its attendant losses. The working atmosphere in these enterprises was characterized by strict discipline and harsh constraints. Both workers and management applied themselves to their jobs chiefly out of fear of losing them. Even then, however, there were a few entrepreneurs who were able to inspire motivation and commitment in their workforce by example!

At that time the aspirations of the workers did not extend much beyond earning a living. Social needs were taken into consideration only occasionally, and only because of the stance adopted by individual entrepreneurs; they did not yet figure on any public agenda. Because of the rapid expansion of industry, this form of liberal capitalism eventually gave rise to some appalling conditions and social conflicts, prompting interventions by the forces of law and order. Influenced by the new conception of man that resulted from the French Revolution, people therefore sought ways of reshaping the world of work.

Politicians initially played the lead role in this process but, as they knew so little about the matters involved, they subsequently decided that the business of drawing up rules for the workplace should be delegated to the unions and the employers' organizations. The representatives of these interest groups came to be known as "tariff partners" [*Tarifpartner*], and the history of how these tariff partners came into being also explains why the term "conflict culture" is used in relation to them—a term borrowed from politics and its system of adversarial parties. As there are different views even today on the merits of conflict culture as a means of forming public opinion, I should like to offer my own assessment of it.

A conflict of different opinions is no doubt helpful as a means of forging a better understanding of complex issues, which is why conflict culture has proved effective in the realm of politics. However, when forming opinions in the context of wage negotiations it needs to be borne in mind that economic decisions almost invariably lie beyond the power of the tariff partners, since the key factors that determine them are not played out within companies themselves, but depend entirely on the choices made by those who buy their products. Responsibility for reacting appropriately to demand must therefore lie solely with the management of each company.

Making changes to people's working conditions is a different matter altogether. Issues that are socially relevant and therefore essentially political cannot really be satisfactorily resolved purely within a company unless outside support is forthcoming, and the tariff partners do indeed come into their own here. Whether the resulting arguments about social issues do them proper justice is highly questionable, however. Whereas in Germany there is much pride in the use of conflict culture as an aid to decision making, not least in the context of the tariff partners and their tussles, other countries are increasingly intent on *reducing* conflict by dealing with problems in an objective manner! With respect to arguments on practical issues between the tariff partners, I, too, am in favor of looking at the problems objectively, and of ensuring that there is a thorough dialogue *within* companies—though I am fully aware that such a procedure can succeed only if it is conducted in a spirit of partnership and fairness!

If on the other hand the tariff partners fail to reach agreement when seeking a solution to social issues, then current, confrontation-based practice leads in the last resort to strikes. It is extremely questionable whether the decisions that result from this outcome are at all appropriate, since it is never the best solution that wins the day, but the superior strength of one or the other party. Just how problematic strikes are as a decision-making mechanism is demonstrated by the efforts of government to head off strikes in the public interest by putting them to arbitration or taking on the role of mediator at round-table discussions. Furthermore, in strike situations the points of contention become so dramatized as the opposing parties battle for supremacy that the working atmosphere in the companies involved remains damaged long after the strike has ended. Although the law lays down that the tariff partners are to cooperate with each other on a basis of trust, there is rarely any sign of such trust once it comes to a strike.

It thus seems to me that in an enterprise culture based on trust and cooperation strikes are the most inappropriate means imaginable for finding a solution that suits all the parties involved. At Bertelsmann we therefore set great store by dialogue and mutual understanding, and regard ourselves as partners in the task of offering the best possible service to society. Our goals and working conditions are agreed upon through a process of dialogue within the company itself and are constantly checked to see if they need to be brought up-to-date. This method of management—entrepreneurial and yet at the same time based on a spirit of partnership—produces results that are accepted and honored by our employees, a fact confirmed by staff surveys. We can therefore confidently assert that it is indeed possible for staff to identify with the company, and that this has enduringly positive results—not only in financial terms, but also in terms of the general atmosphere within the company and the satisfaction level experienced both by the workforce and by those representing capital and management.

Given the contrasting outcomes of these very different decision-making processes, I think it is time to ask ourselves whether our current conception of the tasks now facing us, in the context of new demands on the economy and people's new perception of themselves, should not by sheer force of logic lead us to re-examine and update the task expected of our tariff partners! The extent of the losses currently being caused by strikes is no longer acceptable! In direct contrast to this, the possibility we have of tapping fresh sources of productive energy, thanks to workers identifying with their company, represents a major new opportunity! Given the extent to which Germany has fallen behind with respect to almost all the important performance criteria of our society, it is high time we drew the appropriate conclusions! At Bertelsmann we did this by opting for our enterprise culture, in the firm belief that existing difficulties could be ironed out. So far as the above-mentioned criteria are concerned, our success has very largely proved us right.

One side effect of this enterprise culture that should not be underestimated is the fact that astonishing scope for new management techniques is opened up when all involved in a company fully identify with it, for in these circumstances responsibility can be delegated to the lower levels of the company, and this gives senior management the necessary space to develop their methods and strategies. The quality of management and the results achieved were thereby markedly improved at Bertelsmann, in contrast to the situation in many other large companies, which are clearly doomed to stagnation or insolvency because of their traditional, hierarchical management methods.

By implementing the principle of delegation of responsibility to lower levels we have given our managers and our workforce an opportunity to prove their mettle, and at the same time enabled them to realize more of their potential in professional terms. A particularly remarkable feature of all this is our discovery that it is precisely at the lower levels of the company that very considerable creative potential is to be found—potential that could never come into its own in a hierarchical system.

THE NEED TO SHOW solidarity in the economic realm as much as any other is something that exercised our society throughout almost the whole of the twentieth century. To date, however, we have paid insufficient attention to the complementary concept of "subsidiarity." No democratic system can afford to do without a willingness on the part of its citizens to help themselves (subsidiarity)! Under the enterprise culture system we have successfully given expression to this through our management strategy of delegation.

If the unions argue that Bertelsmann's enterprise culture is an exception and hence not generally applicable, then it has to be admitted that they are not entirely wrong. But what this amounts to is simply a slight delay in a vitally necessary development! For humanizing the world of work is a key factor determining our competitiveness. The sooner we grasp this, the more efficient we will be!

A glance at the way wages and conditions are negotiated in other countries, for instance in Holland or Switzerland, proves that reforms of this sort can indeed be successful. In these countries they decided to take an objective, dispassionate approach to contentious issues, and have discovered that when handled in this way most problems can in fact be resolved at company level!

In this context I should like to add a comment on the practice of codetermination [*Mitbestimmung*]. With regard to this issue, I am well aware that there are many employees in Germany who reject any possibility of dialogue as a matter of principle. On the other hand, we have also seen that getting people accustomed to dialogue within the company builds trust and leads to a willingness to reach a consensus. If we accept that companies will in the future have no choice but to decentralize responsibility on a massive scale, then we should take better note of the fact that the legislation concerning codetermination has also opened up many valuable paths of communication and mutual understanding. Within the ambit of codetermination both sides of the table found themselves actively learning how to cooperate with each other. These outcomes are crucial to the process of creating a way of working that depends on cooperation and mutual understanding: (a) the prerequuisite of good decision making is not conflict culture, but a process of working together and appreciating each other's point of view; (b) particularly in view of the need for responsibility to be delegated to the lower levels of the company, we *have* to be able to rely on both managers and staff identifying with the company's goals. An entrepreneur is expected to have the ability to develop new ideas and bring them to fruition. This being so, it might reasonably be considered one of the great entrepreneurial challenges of the present day to create the circumstances in which staff will identify with their tasks! Several decades ago the American economist and Nobel Prize winner Milton Friedman formulated the provocative thesis that "anything a company does for its workforce over and above what is laid down in wage agreements is a betrayal of its shareholders." I take the opposite view: One of the most pressing entrepreneurial tasks of our time is to invest in the motivation of managers and staff. Such investments bring a very good return.

The new tasks of the tariff partners may be briefly summarized as follows:

1. The increasing complexity of the task of running a business makes it imperative that decision making be decentralized.
2. Investments that encourage the workforce to identify more strongly with their company are a productive contribution to its efficiency and creativity.
3. A management approach based on partnership is the one most likely to engender the requisite cooperative attitude in everyone concerned.

People can have very different opinions about organizational systems and the cultures that tend to accompany them. The "right" solutions vary according to people's basic assumptions about life and their perceptions of themselves. Any new system is ultimately justifiable only if it succeeds—and succeeds not only in economic terms, but also in terms of producing wholehearted acceptance of the way it is organized "on the ground." As I have already mentioned, it takes a long time within the context of workplace culture for people to learn new things, and for new systems to prove themselves. New habits require time, patience, and a willingness to learn!

The issues that we have raised here with regard to management methodology and ways of organizing the economy deserve public attention and need to be debated on an international scale. That being so, I hope to see those in positions of responsibility entering into a constructive dialogue! In any such dialogue we don't want to defend dogmatic positions, but find solutions that are better suited to the requirements of our time and to the way that people today perceive themselves.

FROM CONFLICT CULTURE TO A COOPERATIVE
FORM OF BUSINESS ORGANIZATION

If at all possible, a reform of this sort should not be imposed by the government, but should be developed in a practical context by trying out new forms of cooperation and establishing which of them prove to be effective! This process is facilitated if we avoid making brash, dogmatic announcements, and instead test and evaluate new ways for employers and employees to work in harmony with one another. This approach to developing new methods has been implemented with great success by the Bertelsmann Foundation in hundreds of projects on behalf of the public sector with its very wide range of activities. If the assessment criteria are developed jointly with all the various groups involved, there is a good chance that there will be a sound, objective consensus when it comes to evaluating the results.

This process leading to cooperation and a spirit of partnership in the workplace corresponds far more closely to the way people today perceive themselves. It combines the goal of economic fairness and the desire of employees to help shape the working environment in order to optimize the various processes involved. This constructive grass-roots participation is an essential prerequisite for the future efficiency of a company. Furthermore, the principle of matching pay to performance gives people a good chance of gaining promotion, identifying even more strongly with the company, and achieving more satisfaction in their work. These kinds of reforms of working practices are just as readily accepted by the workforce as, for instance, the introduction of profit sharing for the sake of greater economic fairness. Thus the staff at Bertelsmann are now strongly of the view that it is in their interest to help shape the company in a spirit of partnership. If doubts arise they seek every opportunity to defend this state of affairs and indeed to try out further reforms serving to enhance cooperation and partnership!

In order to establish a solid factual basis for our views on the alternative cultures of "conflict" and " partnership," the Bertelsmann Foundation has begun a comprehensive intercompany comparative study. We measure results that bear on performance such as quantity, value, productivity growth, and staff satisfaction. The results of this are published and discussed in-house. On the basis of our experience so far I would venture the prediction that the representatives of capital, management, and labor will all conclude that an enterprise culture based on partnership is the concept of the future! The Bertelsmann Foundation would be very happy to enter into a dialogue on this issue.

In discussing this kind of process, entrepreneurs will soon discover that it pays to invest in motivation and identification! The unions will find that a cooperative approach within any given company brings additional benefits for employees that would be ruled out on economic grounds if staff and management were at each other's throats. Both sides need time to adjust to reforms such as these which involve changes in both mindset and behavior. I can already confirm from my own experience, however, that the outcome is wholly positive for the company and the individual alike! It has recently been reported in the media that Germany's economic fundamentals have scarcely ever been worse during the whole of its history—and a major contributing factor, in my view, has been the prevalence of "conflict culture" within our economy. Why not therefore try an alternative solution based on the way people today actually see themselves? For once let's have the courage to get rid of the current welter of regulations and instead give people more freedom, reward good performance more vigorously, and both re-quire and enable people to take on more responsibility! Taking as our criteria people's "standard of living," "sense of security," and "level of satisfaction," there are plenty of examples in other coun-tries that prove beyond doubt that subsidiarity and a real sense of involvement in society are more successful than our own attitude toward government, which remains stuck in the past.

THE FUNDAMENTALS OF ENTERPRISE CULTURE

Thanks to education, a higher standard of living, and a greater de-gree of freedom and security, people's perceptions of themselves have changed in such a way that personal aspirations and beliefs play much bigger roles than they did a hundred years ago. People are no longer as vulnerable to poverty and its attendant dangers as they used to be. Forms of social organization such as the family and the ruling class have accordingly changed beyond recognition.

The educational system has reacted to this change by teaching people to develop more independence and to take responsibility for their own lives. This shift from inherited hierarchical structures to flexible and decentralized ones, accompanied by greater empha-sis on the responsibility of the individual, is gathering pace in trade and industry as well as in the public sector, although old habits of mind and the relatively high value still placed on tradition are im-peding this process that is driven by the dictates of the age and people's new perceptions of themselves.

Germany's dangerous inability to reform itself becomes very clear if we take a look at its current ranking relative to the other members of the European Union, where we find that we are low on the list with respect to numerous performance indicators. We ought to realize that we will pay for these omissions by suffering a declining standard of living and a reduction in the state's scope for action.

Whereas international competition and increasingly strong pressure from abroad have forced trade and industry to start taking steps to meet this situation, government policy makers and the state as a whole have scarcely even begun the necessary learning process. Democracy requires that a majority of the electorate support the necessary changes—and at present there is still far too little support for them in Germany. A fair number of those in authority, as well as a large part of the electorate, still think it necessary to hang on to the "achievements" of the past. The argument of "social solidarity" is often used to support this fallacy. Isn't it high time we grasped the fact that it is precisely the goal of solidarity that is put at risk by inflexibility?

Perhaps things have to get still worse for us before even our politicians realize that human beings and their systems must now measure up to global standards. In this context it is a stroke of good fortune that the new perceptions that people have of themselves in Germany and elsewhere are no longer marked by adherence to tradition, but focused instead on the ideal of personal independence, and characterized by the desire to take full advantage of one's opportunities and to try one's luck.

If, thanks to the pressures of competition, the business world is now beginning to recognize how much it needs to learn, then we must find an answer to the question of how the exigencies of management can be brought into accord with the new perceptions that employees have of themselves. The best way of describing this process is to look at some of the business cultures that are emerging today.

In this context it may be useful for us to note a few of the characteristic changes that have occurred in the world of work with respect to the perception of goals and the way in which people behave:

• In earlier days the entrepreneur made all the important decisions himself. His authority was based on his own competence and on strict discipline. Hierarchical structures, however, are no longer capable of transmitting the many kinds of managerial impetus that are necessary today. We have therefore learned that responsibility must be spread across many shoulders, and that people in the lower echelons must also be able to act on their own initiative. This major shift of emphasis in managerial practice requires that staff attitudes to their company be rooted in a strong and genuine sense of identification. The traditional decision-making process based on ownership of a business and effected through hierarchical discipline clearly comes in a very poor second!

• The change in levels of responsibility has major consequences with respect to training, career pathways, and remuneration. Thus, for instance, the leadership abilities of a line manager are just as important today as his technical expertise. In the interests of his own credibility, therefore, a manager must conduct himself in a way that reflects, among other things, an exemplary attitude at the sheerly human level!

• As managers and staff are increasingly expected to make their own individual contributions to their company's success, we must also look at the question of fair remuneration. In the interests of fairness, the principle of performance-related pay should be complemented by various forms of profit sharing!

• Given that enterprise culture attaches special importance to people identifying with the company's aims and enjoying considerable freedom of action, any offense against the company's interests is even graver than it would otherwise be! All staff share in the advantages of such a system, such as social benefits provided over and above the requirements of the law, profit sharing, and secure employment. Any act that damages the interests of the company thus also damages the interests of its employees. Transgressions of this kind must therefore be pursued more vigorously, and to this end there must be continuous close liaison with staff representatives.

• To remain competitive these days, a company needs to be far more flexible in its working methods. However, this flexibility must go hand in hand with the greatest possible stability of employment, since staff understandably regard continuity of employment as the precondition of their sense of motivation and identification. It necessarily follows that a company's strategy and personnel policy must be fully and continuously in harmony, and that safeguarding jobs must be regarded as an important management task.

• The conduct of all of us should be determined by a ready acceptance of, and satisfaction with, our jobs. However, identification with a company's mode of behavior can only occur if an appropriate management style is practiced. The management style best suited to the way people now perceive themselves is that based on partnership.

• For various compelling reasons the state has largely taken over the task of providing a social safety net in Germany. Nonetheless, special cases of need will always arise in any community. Therefore, when such cases are not covered by the state benefit system, a company should step in voluntarily in the interests of its own specific community!

Over the years, the way that goals should be perceived within the private sector has been interpreted in very different ways. This process has unleashed both positive impulses and destructive forces. In our present era, and assuming that it operates on enterprise culture lines, a company should define its goals in a formal constitution in the following terms:

1. The overriding aim of a company is to make its due contribution to society as a whole.
2. While pursuing their own ends, the representatives of management, capital, and labor are nevertheless jointly responsible for fashioning that contribution.
3. Those in charge of the company's management are responsible for coordinating the interests of the various groups and must make their own independent decisions, subject to company rules and policy.

THE GOALS OF THE GROUP REPRESENTATIVES

There is a fixed notion that conflict culture is intrinsic to the dealings of the tariff partners—but in our view of enterprise culture this notion must be countered with the firm and clear assertion that the representatives of capital, management, and labor are all *jointly* responsible for the success of a business. Their responsibilities are as follows:

1. **The entrepreneur** has the ability to spot the opportunities afforded by the marketplace, and to apply his creative flair in such a way as to meet the needs of his customers. He looks for success in the realms of turnover, profitability, and progress. If his management style and his company's commitment to society both meet with approval, then he sees this as clear confirmation that he is doing things right.

2. **Middle management** should be given entrepreneurial conditions of work and should define their goals in the same way as the entrepreneur. Managers throughout the company should enjoy extensive freedom of action within their respective spheres. Their management styles should be such as to make staff feel that they are being treated as partners.

3. **The goals of rank-and-file employees** can no longer be restricted these days to simply earning a living. People's perceptions of themselves today are such that in their jobs they also seek the opportunity to advance and to give real meaning to their lives. Employees should therefore be able to identify with the aims and methods of their company, since this is the essential prerequisite of personal satisfaction, and also of the willingness to take on responsibility. The decisions of management must make good sense, and must be perceived by the workforce as having been arrived at in a spirit of partnership. Remuneration must be commensurate with performance. Enabling staff to share in company profits serves the interests of economic justice and contributes greatly to their sense of motivation. To maintain staff loyalty, staff changes should be kept to a minimum when a company decides to adjust its range of products or services. By making advance preparations for any such adjustments it becomes possible to retain staff and transfer them to new positions. In this way any potential loss of motivation can be minimized, and employees' trust in the company can be reinforced. The "hire and fire" approach so commonly adopted in the United States should not serve as a model for us in Germany.

4. **The goals of capital:** The predominant goals of investors are a decent return and security of investment. The view—once commonly propounded in all the textbooks—that investors are *the* most important factor influencing the economy needs to be

modified these days so that we now describe them as *an* important factor.

Capital cannot always be raised out of a company's own surpluses. The capital market has taken over this function and in the process developed useful criteria for judging the risks and prospective returns of an investment. These criteria are very helpful to banks and borrowers alike when it comes to assessing creditworthiness.

The ready availability of capital is also an important prerequisite of progress today. It is very much to be applauded that whole systems are now being developed to handle capital streams on a global basis. The debate is still ongoing as to what the goals and methods of controlling capital movements should be, and who should be responsible for them. Since putting up capital tends to bring great political power, the interests of the international community require that a solution to this question be found that is socially defensible.

THE RESPONSIBILITY OF THE STATE
IN RELATION TO ECONOMIC POLICY

LESSONS OF THE PAST

History teaches us that uncontrolled striving for power and security can lead to the social status quo becoming completely rigidified. Those who wield power repeatedly fall prey to the illusion that they can secure their power on a long-term basis by invoking tradition and preventing reforms. However, since this is achievable only up to a certain point, regional power monopolies have repeatedly been brought down in the course of history as a result of interventions from within or without. Today we know that only change, constant effort, and a determination to create better social systems can lead us along the one path that promises success, namely the path of enduring competitiveness and an enduring ability to earn a decent living.

A modern society, therefore, obliges the state to be progressive and to embrace systems based on competition and on the efficiency principle. As it lies in the very nature of human beings to seek ever greater power and prestige, anticartel laws have been put in place to prevent monopolies from circumventing or abusing the system within the economic domain—but such constraints are not so easy to achieve in the *public* domain within a society pledged to democracy and to freedom of thought and expression. It is thus the state itself that must ensure that these freedoms are fully safeguarded.

Even in modern democracies, however, we repeatedly find that for all their innovative energies people still fail to instigate the desired progress, or else do so too late, for we all tend to stick doggedly to habits that we have grown fond of. Within a democratic order of things, therefore, there are inevitably recurrent phases of stagnation and undue adherence to the status quo. In such circumstances people's thought processes must be reignited and steered in the direction of progress by their being made aware of alternative possibilities, for instance by the media or by academics. This approach necessarily carries with it the possibility that innovative processes may have adverse consequences; but the interests of progress mean that we cannot simply ban the new out of hand. Only a society that has the courage to take risks and truly desires progress will retain the ability to learn and, in a worst-case scenario, to survive. The task of the responsible authorities in politics and society thus consists not least in keeping the learning process active, and it would do no harm if this goal and the procedures necessary for its realization were to be written into Germany's constitution.

Changed living conditions, new communications technologies, and increasingly specialized education and training have led in recent years to innovations on an unprecedented scale. It behooves us to check very carefully whether our existing structures are capable of providing the kind of direction that society needs. In the economic sphere this challenge can perhaps be met successfully thanks to the competitive pressures mentioned earlier. Whether the state and its politicians are likewise sufficiently capable of learning new things remains to be seen. In this area the pressures for change and for learning new methods have long been totally inadequate. As a result we are lagging seriously behind, and if measures are not taken in the near future to ensure that we catch up, then the next generation will pay a heavy price in the form of a declining standard of living.

NEW GOALS FOR THE STATE

The hierarchical structure and bureaucratic methods of state organizations were an appropriate response two centuries ago to grave shortcomings that were then disfiguring society. The state developed procedures for resolving these problems by using the "best cases" model that is routinely used today, thereby turning best practice into a set of rules that had to be followed at all times. The regulations were drawn up by experts in the field, with due attention being paid to empirical experience. These regulations formed the basis both of the code of practice itself and of the concomitant system of evaluation.

By laying down binding rules, the institutions of the state were able to establish good practice rapidly and on a wide scale, and to set up a comprehensive network for the provision of services. Germany in particular benefited greatly from these arrangements in the nineteenth and twentieth centuries.

During the same period, scholarship, scientific research, and the sharing of experience with countries abroad brought a massive expansion of knowledge unprecedented in history. This torrent of new knowledge, however, was assimilated only partially and hesitantly by the apparatus of the state. And once the state had decided to modify any of its procedures, it insisted that the new one be followed to the very letter. The annual review of the various areas of responsibility within the state is essentially concerned only with checking that the rules have been adhered to, that all procedures are fully in accordance with regulations. In periods of rapid change, however, this practice often inhibited progress over long stretches of time, since rules that made good sense when they were originally introduced often turn into a brake on progress! This rigid and obstructive system of administration ultimately caused the competence of the state to be called into question, and led to the alternative remedy of privatizing the various functions.

Because of this extremely sluggish pace of reform—something that only a monopolistic organization can get away with for any length of time—the state ended up becoming ever less responsive to the interests of its citizens! But instead of realizing that freedom, plurality, and competition have become indispensable impulses within our society, we are continuing our traditional habit of trusting blindly in the state, and are thereby running the risk of failing to meet the challenges of the present day.

Most leading figures in trade and industry find it incomprehensible that our democratic institutions operate in such a ponderous way. The claim that the principles of efficiency and competition cannot be applied to the realm of politics and the state is in truth merely an unthinking prejudice on the part of those who are determined to preserve the status quo! For in a period of global competition and change, what matters most is not discipline and adherence to the rules, but creativity, relevance, efficiency, and identification with the job—in a word: competitiveness!

To many of our politicians and public servants this approach to management is still entirely alien. The fiasco at the Federal Labor Office (*Bundesanstalt für Arbeit*) that made headlines in the spring of 2002 is a typical example. Nonetheless, the parties sought in the election to appease the voters with lavish promises—though this did not stop the public clamor for transparency and comprehensibility from becoming ever more insistent. Thanks not least to the intervention of former Federal President Roman Herzog, who attacked the antiquatedness of the state's management methods and called for reforms, it has become crystal clear that the political leadership's way of working is seriously behind the times.

The problems created by change have provoked an entirely different reaction in most of the private sector. Management has become far more difficult as a result of the sheer quantity of work and the new demands that people face, and companies have met the challenge by adopting the principle that we have already discussed on several previous occasions, namely that of delegating responsibility right down to the lowest echelons. In so doing, full account was taken of the fact that this new system of management can only succeed if everyone given such responsibility identifies with his job. The following imperatives emerge from this tried-and-tested strategy, all of which must also be taken to heart by those in the political domain:

- Responsibility should be delegated downward to the fullest possible extent.
- The government must set performance-based goals, and must have the courage to try new things! All tasks must be defined in such a way that they are measurable.

- Personnel policy must be so designed that remuneration and opportunities for promotion fully reflect the abilities of each individual.
- Working conditions in the public sector must be brought into line with those in the private sector.
- The goal of public service must in future be defined as "progress and competitiveness" instead of "adherence to the rules."

The astonishing effect that identification and motivation have on the sense of commitment of employees is made very clear by these statistics from the Federation of Company Health Schemes (*Bundesverband der Vertriebskrankenkassen*):

ANNUAL STATISTICS FOR ABSENCE FROM WORK
(sick leave)

Area of activity	No. of days absent	Reduction in efficiency[3]
State[1]	28	9%
Industry[1]	16	5%
Bertelsmann AG[1]	12	4%
Well-run subsidiaries of Bertelsmann AG[2]	2–5	1–2%
Difference between badly run and well-run organizations		Circa 7–8 % reduction in efficiency

[1] Source: Federation of Company Health Schemes.
[2] Source: Bertelsmann AG.
[3] Ratio of days of absence to total number of workable days.

The difference in the number of days of absence is not due to a greater or lesser workload, but to the extent of an employee's sense of identification with the goals and management style of the organization concerned. Organizations that are run according to enterprise culture principles achieve a high degree of identification and a matching willingness to put in a good day's work. In contrast to this, organizations that are run on hierarchical, bureaucratic lines forfeit on average 7 to 8 percent of their potential productivity.

A survey of worker motivation undertaken by Gallup Germany shows a similar picture. According to Gallup, the attitude of German workers to their jobs breaks down as follows:

committed	15%
uncommitted	69%
deliberately uncommitted	16%

Gallup claims that this lack of commitment causes economic damage to the tune of 221.1 billion euros per annum.

The key factor determining the level of motivation and the working atmosphere in an organization is the way it is managed! Enterprise culture is based on an awareness of this nexus. This not only applies to the private sector—it applies even more strongly to the public sector, given the latter's questionable approach to management!

In order to fully understand the effects of motivation we need to appreciate that it not only enhances people's willingness to work, but it has an equally positive effect on quality, reliability, and cooperativeness! My thesis that enterprise culture plays a key role in giving a company a competitive edge is borne out in plain and simple terms by the above-mentioned sources.

This nexus ought to be recognized by those in commanding positions in government and the economy, and they should draw the appropriate conclusions. The potential for improvement can easily be ascertained by getting all staff to fill in a questionnaire. There are hidden reserves of profitability here that give pause for thought even to hardened devotees of shareholder value! It needs to be emphasized that improvements of this kind have a very beneficial effect on the level of satisfaction felt by employees. The various key elements of enterprise culture with its new management technique thus contribute significantly to the stability and continuity of our society.

It is not yet clear how politicians will respond to the incontrovertible fact that their way of running things is seriously behind the times, nor is it clear how we are going to get ourselves on track to bring about the necessary reforms. At least it must have become apparent to us by now that our customary election-time strategy of pandering to voters represents a mode of "leadership" that has very little to do with the essential notions underlying democracy. Furthermore, one is left gasping at the sheer brazenness of our politicians in handing out money that they don't even have at their disposal! A further mortal sin of politicians is their dogged adherence to hierarchical structures. Germany, more than any other country, has proved through its history that hierarchical systems are a most unsuitable way of trying to safeguard the future. In the past we have found again and again that the only things that offer a real prospect of success are efficiency, a capacity for change, and leaders whose suitability for their job is proven beyond doubt. We can certainly understand the attitude of those in the public sector who cling to the status quo: After all, to have risen to an office of some importance is flattering and a source of prestige and respect. Where different systems are in competition with one another, however, success does not derive from flattering people's vanity. For the sake of our citizens, and for the sake of our democracy's ability to function effectively, the following principles must be attended to:

1. Subsidiarity must rate just as highly in our country as solidarity.

2. The demand for transparency in all dealings within the public sector must also be effected through an efficient information system and through regularly updated comparisons with corresponding practices in other countries.

3. Only a long-term program of further training and of nurturing potential management talent can guarantee success and continuity. This also applies to political parties and state organizations!

4. Only when the political and public sector elites have already proved themselves according to performance-oriented criteria should the democratic selection process come into play.

5. Given the increasing difficulty of management, we have to establish career profiles for politics and the public sector that will be attractive to highly talented candidates. There are no rational grounds for letting most of the best people take themselves off to other sectors! Better candidates need to be recruited if the task of political leadership is to be carried out effectively and in a way that serves the public interest!

If critics—especially from among the ranks of our politicians—object that there is simply no money for a personnel program of this kind, then they should reflect on the fact that when businesses fail it is almost always because of incompetent management. Things are no different in the public sector! Savings on staff are therefore always false savings. Our lack of money is the result of our inability to bring our democracy up-to-date and, more particularly, to train and retain suitable managers!

Paying good people good money is always worth it! Envy at the grass-roots level can be more easily appeased if those in charge do a demonstrably good job. All major businesses that have organized themselves on performance-oriented lines are familiar with this problem, and make provisions for it. There is thus no excuse for the failure of politicians!

IS THE ENTERPRISE CULTURE APPROACH
TO MANAGEMENT TRANSFERABLE?

Now that it is becoming ever more apparent that the enterprise culture system is superior to all other management models within the private sector, the question arises whether this method can also be applied within the public sector with its very wide range of different tasks. I have already described the shortcomings of the hierarchical, bureaucratic method of management. I would add that the experience of other countries clearly demonstrates that a great many services currently provided by the state can be taken over by the private sector—who indeed achieve greater success with respect to both quality and value for money.

If we therefore now face the question of changing from one system to another, it is necessary to weigh the advantages and disadvantages of such a far-reaching decision. In doing so, we are not really concerned with the issue of privatizing state-run activities, but rather with the question of whether a performance-driven enterprise culture can be successfully applied *within* the existing state-run system—thus introducing competition into the public sector!

The disadvantages of the state's approach to management are unmistakable. The state accounts for approximately 45 percent of our national product! This statistic alone shows that reform is urgently necessary. Given that we cannot rationalize *all* the functions of the state—such as the administration of justice, for instance— our search for a practicable alternative centers on the following questions:

1. Which functions can be privatized?
2. Is it possible to run public service on a competitive basis?
3. Should enterprise culture methods be introduced into the political and public service domains?

Given the astonishing successes I have seen in my own experience of the enterprise culture system, readers will not be surprised to hear that my emphatic recommendation is that it should indeed be introduced into the public sector!

I should like to underpin this recommendation with a series of questions and answers, as follows:

Question I

What would citizens rate more highly, "the same services for everyone," or "better services for everyone"? If people were able to vote on this question, I have no doubt as to the outcome! The realities of a market economy have made them extremely familiar with this issue! In underdeveloped countries the argument that things should be the same for everyone used to hold considerable attraction; people there viewed profit-oriented market economies with great skepticism. Today, however, our citizens expect the democratic apparatus itself to perform efficiently, and to do so on the basis of competitiveness!

Question 2

What is more important in the economic realm, size or competitiveness? Our citizens know perfectly well that cost savings can be achieved by increasing production volumes. But on the other hand they have also seen large companies go bankrupt because they weren't sufficiently flexible. Now of course our public service sector is more than big enough to achieve the economies of scale that we might theoretically expect. In practice, however, our citizens can readily see that other countries, and indeed private service providers within our own country, are considerably more efficient. They are slowly coming to realize that size is *not* the crucial factor, but rather competitiveness, creativity, and flexibility are. These criteria, however, are evidently still not sufficiently appreciated by those who wield political power.

Question 3

Does raw competition within the economic sphere provide sufficient impetus on its own, or do our citizens want the state to give the system a humane dimension? Enterprise culture offers an answer to this question that chimes very clearly with the way people today perceive themselves.

In the public as in the economic sphere, enterprise culture is an organizational system that hinges on freedom, understanding, and identification, not compulsion, discipline, and punishment! These days the top echelons of major organizations—which include government ministries—simply can no longer handle all the decisions that are necessary to guarantee progress! The sluggish pace of reform is a characteristic result of this dismal state of affairs. Many major organizations here have meanwhile realized that they can make decisions much more effectively by delegating responsibility.

By way of example I would mention those concerns that operate globally by means of a decentralized structure, and I should also like to mention the new management techniques used by the armed forces! By these means, numerous state-run activities have been opened up once again to the benefits of progress—particularly in the English-speaking countries.

Under the aegis of the enterprise culture system the learning opportunities that are now available are put to the best possible use, since by building on the staff's strong sense of identification these opportunities enable the principle of delegated responsibility to be realized on a large scale. As a result it is not only the Executive Board that has scope to make decisions but also middle management and staff in general. Problems need to be solved more effectively in *all* areas of a company or indeed of the state, and no form of management is better at this task than enterprise culture!

With good reason and complete conviction I therefore strongly recommend that the huge untapped potential of the people's powers of identification and commitment be activated by the introduction of enterprise culture! If this is successfully carried out we will one day be able to exult in the triumph of humane values!

5

ENTERPRISE CULTURE AS A CONTRIBUTION TO DEMOCRACY?

THE NEW SELF-PERCEPTION OF THE CITIZEN

The simplest form of leadership is untrammeled authoritarian rule, which often occurs when a society first begins to take shape. But the more complicated the demands on the leadership of a society become, the clearer it becomes that hierarchical structures are unsuited to dealing with complex control processes.

The Germans had to find this out the hard way in the twentieth century. After the collapse of the Nazi regime, and with the help of the Allies, we embarked on the politically more demanding path of establishing a democracy, and in this we made enormous progress. Nonetheless, we only have to look, for instance, at the blind faith that most people still have in the state to see how deeply our thinking is still influenced by the hierarchical habits of previous eras. Many Germans still take the view that it is the state's job to sort things out when anything goes wrong. By contrast, it is not always appreciated that in our era more than in any other it is the very fact that the state apparatus and its capacity for management are seriously overstretched that chiefly accounts for our inability to cope with the implacable process whereby systems have to change and evolve.

Fortunately, however, democratically ordered societies give people plenty of scope to learn from their mistakes. This learning process, though, does not kick in first among those elected representatives who fill the top positions in government, who are often overburdened, and who have only a very nebulous sense of what is gravely amiss in their society. Instead, it is people at the grass-roots level who first experience its detrimental effects, since they are personally affected by the consequences of wrong decisions. Clear examples of this are the labor market and the health system! Only when the defects in the state system become unbearably oppressive for the voters do things begin to change once the political parties start competing with one another to introduce reforming ideas.

This kind of time lag occurs, incidentally, not only in the political and public administration sphere, but is also alarmingly evident in certain major organizations in the private sector. This turn of events quite often culminates not in a learning process, but in the collapse of the company together with all the grave social consequences that this entails!

Many businesses have therefore adopted the above-mentioned principle of the delegation of responsibility, and this is strongly to be recommended in the context of politics and society as well. My advice is that the process should begin at the grass-roots level, since ordinary citizens are not only directly affected by bad rules and regulations, but they also often possess such sound judgment that they can offer useful advice or can themselves assume responsibility for sorting out the problem.

When thinking about the question of how best to get people to give their services to the state and to the economy, it is helpful to draw a comparison between examples taken from the two different realms, namely "civil society" and "enterprise culture." At the political level, the kind of civil society that is familiar to us in the English-speaking world makes a very efficient contribution to the educational process within a properly functioning democracy. The system works because people feel fully involved in human terms and fully committed as citizens. It responds quickly, economically, and humanely. This kind of arrangement, too, requires a consensus, but this consensus is more easily achieved since the people concerned have a better grasp of the situation! If we look back in history, incidentally, we find that a similar tradition of taking on tasks in the public domain already existed centuries ago in Germany in the shape of the citizens' associations commonly found in smaller towns. For my own forebears it went without saying that they would donate part of their time and energy to their community. If we were to follow this same path again today, Germany would be governed more effectively and more economically, and would have fewer problems with excessively sluggish reforms!

The second example I mentioned was "enterprise culture." The problems posed by size, and by the need for people to open their minds to new possibilities, are just as pressing in the economy as they are in the state sector. There is now such a plethora of complex tasks that they can no longer all be dealt with solely by the top echelon of an organization. If the private sector has made more progress than the public sector in solving these problems, it is because of the pressure of competition, which can sometimes threaten the very existence of a company. Compared to this, our political representatives still lead pretty comfortable lives, even when they are in opposition!

In the private sector, reducing the burden on top management is a matter of existential importance, given that a company's success or failure can depend on it. It would also be helpful if the managers involved were better qualified—but that on its own would not suffice! Rather, we must develop our present management methodology in such a way that we can transfer responsibility from the top to as many people as possible on the lower tiers of management. This process of delegating responsibility is not only difficult but dangerous, for if the people who acquire new responsibilities set their own interests above the goals of the company, then traits such as greed, power seeking, or simply the need to feel important can cause the collapse not only of the principle of delegation but of the company itself. Egocentric agendas of this kind on the part of senior managers—very familiar to us from the past, but still all too common today—represent a grave obstacle on the road to a new enterprise culture, since this culture presupposes exemplary behavior, a strong degree of identification, and, not least, the relinquishing of personal interests!

Taking a global view, we have to recognize that the current expansion of the capitalist system has reached a certain limit, dictated not only by the greatly increased difficulties entailed by the sheer task of management, but also by the resistance it encounters within society. Academics and other theoreticians have not yet come up with an adequate answer to the problem of how to synthesize the goals of the various interest groups. The heated arguments about aims and management methodologies within the economy and economic policy stem very largely from this failure to redefine our goals.

As businesses grow in size, so their goals and management philosophy increasingly take on a social dimension—and this is why the enterprise culture system, together with the principle of delegation, is capable of solving the problems relating to size and (lack of) progress not only in the private sector but also in the public sector. Enterprise culture presupposes that all those involved in an enterprise identify fully with it, and by virtue of their involvement and the ideas that they generate it improves the political leadership's capacity for action and makes it easier to modernize the social system.

SELF-FULFILLMENT WITHIN THE WORLD OF WORK

In the early days of industrialization the task of a worker amounted to what was later termed the "labor factor." Jobs were relatively simple and could be carried out equally well by unskilled workers. In these circumstances it was possible to set up mass production plants at breathtaking speed, and thanks to low taxes and the initial paucity of competition, it was also possible to meet capital requirements out of profits. Practically nothing remains of these givens of early capitalism—not even in the developing countries!

Today, international competition is all about the relative advantages of products and systems. In place of the brute "labor factor" we have the immense potential of highly qualified specialist workers and managers. And even those representing the "capital factor" no longer play this role thanks only to the sheer magnitude of their wealth, but also because of their skill in putting their capital to work.

The complete change in the nature of the task that workers were required to perform not only demanded new skills, it also led them to perceive themselves in a different way and to embrace an entirely new set of goals—a development that was only slowly recognized as the industrialization process went on. Even today, insufficient account is taken of its consequences, which have caused the function of the entrepreneur to evolve into two distinct roles: that of supplying capital and that of managing the business.

In conjunction with these changes, the period since the French Revolution has seen the emergence of a new conception of man, and a new understanding of the processes of social change driven by political parties and unions within a democracy. In the course of the last two centuries this change in the way people perceived themselves resulted in labor disputes that were no longer simply about securing a basic standard of living, but were also about enabling people to achieve greater self-fulfillment in the world of work. It was a stroke of good fortune that this development happened to coincide with the various pressures forcing managers to decentralize responsibility!

Because of the increasing difficulty of the tasks involved, however, it was not long before many unskilled workers proved unable to meet the requirements for being given decision-making powers in the work process. Intensive theoretical and practical training and experience proved to be an indispensable prerequisite for the careers people chose, and this trend has culminated in the present-day need for the learning process to continue throughout an individual's life! Business and government have both shared responsibility for professional qualifications, but labor-market policies in particular demonstrate very clearly that there is a third and equally responsible party, namely the individual worker himself! For without sufficient interest, willingness, and personal involvement on his part, the various training and qualification programs available would meet with precious little success! As this pattern develops, it is already becoming evident at shop-floor level that there is a category of workers who will remain on the bottom tier of the labor-market pyramid because of their lack of adequate qualifications. Our society must see to it that sufficient work at an appropriate wage is available for these people, too! This will scarcely be feasible, however, without a very great degree of flexibility in the labor market.

The varying levels of ability and efficiency among those involved in the work process must be taken into account, partly to ensure the company's success, but also to ensure that the workforce remains satisfied and feels that it all makes sense. It is important that *all* staff support the goals of the company, and that for the sake of fairness they be enabled to share in the company's success! This objective must also be reflected in the company's management style with its emphasis on partnership: Line managers must make every effort to help their staff to develop their potential and understand the whys and wherefores of the company's directives.

That work is more than just a necessary evil is regarded by psychologists these days as self-evidently true. Work not only enables people to earn their bread but also gives them personal satisfaction and lends meaning to their lives, especially when it goes beyond merely enabling them to keep body and soul together and is oriented to the needs of the community at large. Work, too, must find due recognition, and must serve to boost our self-confidence! The democratic system enables every citizen to try his luck—but it also requires him to do his bit and to make his contribution to the commonweal.

Every citizen should accordingly develop a long-term plan for his life—partly to ensure that he can earn his living, but also with a view to achieving maximum self-fulfillment. A real sense of satisfaction after a fulfilled life doesn't, after all, reside simply in the knowledge that one has "made it" and achieved wealth and distinction; instead, it grows out of the feeling that in addition to securing our own material existence we have also contributed to the well-being of others.

THE SLUGGISH PACE OF REFORM
IN THE PUBLIC SECTOR

Germany's inability and unwillingness to keep pace with the new self-perception of its citizens and the new management techniques now available may perhaps still be due to the once common belief that it is possible to devise optimal processes and procedures that will remain so no matter how much times may change.

In the old days, after all, everyone—rulers and ruled alike—were convinced that their traditions were permanent and, within the limitations of human nature, both "fair" and "humane." In the largely static systems of the preindustrial era no change of any significance ever occurred, apart from the emergence of new dynasties and their representatives.

The deficiencies in management technique that this gave rise to were at least partly offset by the initiative of the wealthier citizens, who frequently devoted part of their time and a very considerable part of their fortune to charitable works by helping to fund nursery schools, elementary schools, high schools, hospitals, and orphanages, and maintaining welfare associations. Even today, countless charitable organizations in towns throughout the country bear witness to their citizens' sense of commitment.

Thanks to these initiatives the worst of the shocking conditions prevailing at the time were alleviated, albeit only within the ambit of the larger towns. It was only much later that the state took on the responsibility of providing all the most important social services on a systematic and comprehensive basis. The fact that civil society then made no further progress in Germany was chiefly due to the continued existence of hierarchical social structures, though it was also partly due to the tempestuous pace of industrialization. The dire poverty of the working class called for urgent measures, which had to come into effect far more quickly than was possible through the gradual evolution of a full-scale learning process. The path that was chosen was accordingly not that of initiatives undertaken by citizens themselves within their own communities, but that of a massive enlargement of the administrative apparatus of the state, since this was seen as the only feasible solution to the problem.

At the same time, however, the new developments in education and technology gave people much greater scope to shape their lives as they wished, and this was further encouraged by the palpable process of democratization, improvements in the standard of living, a more comprehensive communications network, and the rapidly expanding opportunities for contacts with other countries. Since traditional social structures were plainly incapable of accommodating the new assumptions and expectations on which people sought to build their lives, they increasingly turned their back on the rules of the past and attempted to develop new systems of their own. Thus began a painful process of reshaping society—a process that is still in full swing today! On the one side we see the representatives of progress and humane values, and on the other the dogmatists and those determined to preserve the status quo.

Under these circumstances, how does a society arrive at a social order that is both forward looking and acceptable to its citizens?

Should we, in an act of blind faith, simply adopt the systems of others? Or are these systems, too, destined for the scrap heap because of the rapid pace of change? To judge by everything that the last two hundred years have taught us, the process of change will be with us for a very long time to come. Many innovations have still by no means realized their full potential. On the contrary, their effects are just beginning to reveal themselves. One only has to think of the education and health systems, for instance, or the overall systems of democracy and the market economy! No one can seriously maintain that our present systems have already reached their final form, perfectly attuned to the prevailing circumstances and the nature of mankind; but fortunately we have at least come to realize that the systems and aspirations of the past can lay no claim to enduring validity. This is an insight that holds much promise for the future. But how, then, are we to find our way forward? Do we have the right aims? Can we rely on having a secure existence in the future as well as in the present? And what do we ourselves need to contribute in order to ensure that change becomes progress? Is it helpful to bear in mind that the "less bad" option is never the good one? Or should we let the competition principle point the way? Are there pointers that will show us the way not just to renewed greatness and power, but also to a more humane order?

With regard to the sluggish pace of reform in our society, we can pose the following question on the basis of the above-mentioned insights: In order to trigger the kind of social progress that is potentially within our grasp, have we already introduced the requisite degree of competition into all our various systems? Or could it be that this issue has still not been seriously confronted?

IS IT POSSIBLE TO IDENTIFY WITH THE STATE?

The management system best suited to the working conditions prevalent in today's economy, namely enterprise culture, can function only if all involved identify with the aims of the organization. Should we seek to create this situation within the context of the state, too?

European history over the last two centuries was characterized by a sustained effort to make the change from hierarchical social structures to a system of democracy. Given the often chaotic nature of the learning process throughout this period, one could scarcely claim that people in general identified with the state. The goals and behavior patterns of rulers and ruled were too different from each other for this to be possible, and the various regimes were too dogmatic in orientation. The rules and regulations decreed by the state were therefore frequently challenged, not to mention actively opposed!

In recent times we have also discovered that people can be very easily manipulated! Since the instruments of manipulation take many forms and are not even recognized as such by their victims, it is no wonder that entire nations blindly followed their rulers into the abyss. The Germans' involvement in the crimes of the Nazi regime is a particularly shocking example of this.

Identification with the state can therefore only be expected if the state in question is rooted in freedom and democracy, is primarily concerned with respecting human dignity rather than achieving mere "efficiency," and has systems appropriate to people's self-perception and to the constantly evolving circumstances of modern life! We cannot bring our systems up-to-date simply by following orders handed out to us by our "rulers," instead we must all assume some responsibility and make a positive contribution, each according to his own abilities and place in life!

The Bertelsmann Foundation has availed itself with great success of every opportunity to make comparison-based evaluations of performance in respect to all public sector undertakings. There is enormous scope at the present time for learning from performance evaluations! Given its history, Germany must now learn above all that hierarchies in politics and the state serve only to slow things down! In all those tasks that call for solutions and action, we need more decentralization, more freedom, more flexibility, more transparency. And as the various systems vie with one another, we as citizens can more readily identify with what we ourselves have been responsible for. We shall then work more thriftily and do our very best to make progress a reality.

It is therefore no longer sufficient these days to limit our personal involvement in the democratic system to turning up to vote in elections every now and again; as citizens we must instead feel personally responsible for our society and act accordingly! This applies to all areas of society, from our families and jobs to the apparatus of the state. If we succeed in acting according to this principle, then we will be able to put an end to the sluggish pace of reform in Germany and also to liberate our very considerable creative potential.

6

MANAGING THE STATE AND MANAGING A BUSINESS: SOME COMMON FEATURES

SOME PROPOSITIONS ON THE SOCIAL SIGNIFICANCE OF CHANGE

While the principle of competition is increasingly under-stood and implemented in the world's economies, this is by no means the case in those areas of activity for which the state is responsible. In a situation where there is global competition between different systems, however, it will soon be necessary for states to show real progress if they are to retain their political and even their cultural independence—*especially* the latter. This being so, I should like once again to outline the importance of competition by presenting a number of propositions in which I shall also demonstrate why competition has made scarcely any headway in the public sector.

1. Societies were formed originally on the basis of power.
2. Those in power were chiefly interested in maintaining their own status, and shaped the political culture of their society accordingly.
3. Progress never figured among the aims of the powerful; indeed it was often regarded by them as a potential threat. Rulers expected to gain no advantage whatever from change.
4. In relatively stable times it was therefore possible for the belief to become firmly established that society should hold fast to its inherited political and social culture.
5. However, the change in the material conditions of life that occurred over the last couple of centuries in Europe have led people to perceive themselves quite differently.
6. The rulers' sheer possession of power was no longer seen as sufficient to justify their exercise of it. People began to realize that *competence* is the sole justification for anyone becoming a leader!
7. Only when democratization began to set in did people start systematically challenging the goals and methods of their rulers, and their fitness for office. As a result, progress replaced continuity as the goal of society.
8. Increased knowledge and greater liberty enable us today to make comparisons between different systems. In seeking to improve the way the state runs things we should take careful account of the results of international competition, and by making such comparisons we can profit from the wide range of solutions devised by countries around the world.
9. Just as the principle of competition has proved its worth as the motor driving progress within the private sector, so too in

the public sector we now have tools for measuring and evaluating performance. Using these tools to measure success could easily trigger a massive cultural shift. "Competitiveness" will be the order of the day instead of "sticking to the rules." This offers the possibility of a continuous process of evolutionary change!

10. It is already apparent, however, that in the public sector, too, the way forward must not be determined solely by sheer political majorities: Full account must also be taken of solutions that have proved themselves in the context of international competition.

11. This approach to bringing our systems up-to-date does not conflict with the principles of democracy or of a market economy. Instead, it is an indispensable learning process serving to strengthen and protect our society, and at the same time it will bring a marked improvement in the way our democratic system functions.

12. The fact that we are only now beginning to realize this is probably due to the attitude of politicians, who even today show relatively little interest in seeing their performance subject to proper evaluation. Furthermore, we have not until now had the tools available to us for measuring performance in the public sector and thereby introducing competition.

Summary

Looking at the example of how the private sector has developed as a result of competition, we can also identify the following principles:

• Political progress will scarcely be achievable in a democracy—at any rate *within* the system—unless decentralization is introduced on a large scale.

• Abortive social developments can be rapidly identified as such if *all* developments are carried out with complete transparency.

• Most economic functions cannot be replicated by state monopolies with the same measure of success.

• In the private sector the respective roles played by the representatives of capital, management, and labor must be in accord with the imperatives of international competition. If any of these groups achieves a monopolistic position, political intervention may be required to ensure the continued viability of the system.

In periods of change the consequences of increased competition cannot be met solely by bringing management techniques up-to-date and relying on the provisions of anti-trust legislation. If the economy is to serve humanity, then a careful eye must be kept on the potential repercussions when an organization becomes very large and hence very powerful.

THE PRIVATE SECTOR MUST HELP THE STATE

We know from experience that in other countries as well as in Germany, those who wield power show astonishingly little interest in bringing their management methods up-to-date. They feel that the law as it stands gives them ample legitimacy. And indeed, provided they don't actually infringe these laws, any inquiry into their actions will declare them to be in keeping with the rules and regulations and therefore completely in order.

This practice can scarcely be deemed appropriate, however, once we acknowledge that in these changing times, new circumstances should lead us to devise new ways of running things. Many of our elected representatives, however, clearly believe that their decisions are invariably correct, and so they never even consider alternative strategies or the possibility of updating the rules—for those who govern a state founded on the rule of law think they *are* the law!

This mentality is almost incomprehensible to business leaders and entrepreneurs used to responding to competition and used to performance-driven management. There is ample proof that our public sector system is not competitive—and that it meets with approval among the population. This state of affairs is barely even touched on in elections, and even the opposition is often incapable of attacking mistaken ideas.

The only possible inference to be drawn from this is that the public sector—which in Germany devours almost half the gross national product—is not subject to the requisite forces in respect to its efficiency. The counterargument that the political parties' conflict culture will in due course bring an end to this monstrous state of affairs is scarcely reassuring, and has never been convincingly proved. The truth of the matter is that our political parties are interested first and foremost in power; reform is a secondary issue. Reversing this order of priorities would produce better results!

I would therefore like to raise the question of whether our business leaders shouldn't be more willing to see it as their responsibility to challenge the goals and working practices now prevalent in the public sector, and to help politicians and the state to adopt the performance-driven methods of management that are available today. That way we would not only save money, but above all we would learn very rapidly that there are management techniques in existence that can modernize our systems from within.

WHO CARRIES RESPONSIBILITY
FOR THE LABOR MARKET?

At the end of the Second World War Germany's towns and cities lay in ruins—and so, too, did the majority of the country's businesses. Many businesses had to start from scratch again, and in the process they had dire firsthand experience of the limitations of a state-run economy. Anyone sticking to the state's rules in those days would scarcely have been able to earn a crust, let alone achieve economic success! This coercive economy only came to an end with Ludwig Erhard's currency reform of June 1948—which within an astonishingly short period of time caused both the economy and society in general to burst into new life in a way that scarcely anyone would have considered possible. Quite literally overnight, goods and services suddenly became available again. The world was amazed, and spoke of the "German economic miracle."

In the following decades, too, Germany's social market economy proved to be a remarkable success. It wasn't until the 1970s that politicians started putting extra tax burdens on the private sector in the name of social progress—which meant trying to win over voters and thus win elections with the lure of new services. Now, however, we have reached the point where a mass of rules and regulations have so thoroughly stifled the driving forces of the marketplace and of performance orientation that Germany is now coming a poor last in comparison with the rest of Europe.

So far as the labor market is concerned, our politicians have given the administrative apparatus of the state a task that it simply cannot cope with! The whole apparatus of the state is effectively incapable of learning anything new, since its goals are not performance driven, and it is not subject to the pressures of competition. What we need, however, is people experienced in performance-driven management and, above all, open to learning new ways of doing things. The German labor market does not present any unusual problems. The same kinds of problems have long been dealt with more effectively by other countries—and we could learn from them!

If this doesn't happen, perhaps because we imagine that we will achieve better results if we do things "the German way," then it will be sheer irresponsibility on our part. It is thus very much to be welcomed that politicians in their current state of helplessness are turning to the private sector for advice. But there is still insufficient appreciation of where the real challenge lies, namely complete reform of labor market policies! What is certain at any rate is that the measures taken so far will *not* lead to a second German economic miracle!

One interesting question in this context is the extent to which business leaders can make up for the weaknesses of the government's labor market policies by making use of their freedom of action within their own companies and hence within the economy as a whole. What is certain is that the failings of government policy cannot *all* be remedied by actions taken within the business sector. But provided that business leaders can see their goals from a social as well as economic perspective, much could be done to improve things with respect to the miserable phenomenon of unemployment.

I should like to offer a few propositions on this topic:

1. Business leaders today must bear in mind how important *motivation* is for performance and success! If motivation is undermined

in any way, this reduces the company's level of performance and hence its competitiveness! The workforce must be able to identify with the company!

2. In times of change companies cannot always avoid having to lay off workers. Implementation of a long-term personnel policy fully coordinated with the company's overall strategy can, however, soften the blow for workers affected by significant changes of direction or emphasis within the company, for instance by offering part-time work, retraining, or help in finding a new job.

3. In the past, business leaders have regarded it as the state's responsibility to ensure that the labor market operates effectively. Today they could easily take much of this responsibility into their own hands! The same applies—only much more emphatically—to the "tariff partners" who, by agreeing to settlements heavy with provisos, conditions, and rules, are at present severely constricting the creative potential of the economy.

4. The enterprise culture method of management makes it possible to reform and reshape the labor market in decisive ways—not least because enterprise culture can minimize losses due to industrial unrest, while also increasing efficiency because the goals and general behavior of the company have the support of its employees! What was achieved in 1948 by introducing a social market economy can be achieved again in our own time by implementing a humane enterprise culture!

ELEMENTS NEEDED FOR CREATING A COMPETITIVE SYSTEM IN THE PUBLIC SECTOR

In order to outline the elements that competitiveness depends on, I offer the following propositions:

1. Alongside the principle of "adherence to the rules," the principle of *maximum efficiency* must be applied to all activities! Reduced productivity results in inferior services for the citizen!

2. Just as our democracy sticks up for solidarity, so too it must support subsidiarity, i.e., the notion that citizens themselves should deal with everything that lies within their powers and abilities. Reducing state involvement to an absolute minimum: This is a principle we must insist on in Germany, too!

3. It is often the people within the community who from their own personal experience know best what kind of help is needed and how methods can be improved. The state should make use of this knowledge and call on people to involve themselves directly in their communities!

4. *All* activities within the ambit of state-run services can be structured in such a way that they can be measured against specific performance criteria. Criteria of this kind must also be developed for all full-time employees of the state with a view to assessing their efficiency and establishing a basis for determining their pay.

5. A comparison of different performance levels achieved in similar activities can be used in a competition-based system to assess the standard attained in any particular case, and at the same time identify any scope for improvement. All employees of the state should be informed that any substantial increase in pay has to be based on an increase in the state's productivity.

6. Where the performance of state-run activities is compared on an international basis, the comparison must also include average values in the private sector, and must likewise include equivalent activities in other countries.

7. Some form of profit sharing based on performance makes sound sense in the state sector, and is readily feasible.

8. Within the private sector, fair dealing and plentiful opportunities for staff involvement in decision making have brought about a high degree of motivation and identification with the job—factors that have a far more positive effect on worker efficiency than, for instance, obedience and discipline! This latent energy should be tapped, in exactly the same way, in the public sector as well!

9. Progress requires innovation and the discovery of new ways of doing things. Even staff and their supervisors in the lowest ranks of an organization should be enabled to incorporate their fund of experience into the work process, and should be rewarded for any ensuing success. Scope for innovation and for trying out and/or learning new ways of doing things should therefore be provided more particularly at the lower levels of responsibility. In the long run it is far cheaper for the community to try out reforms than to stick rigidly to time-honored habits.

10. Any additional calls on public sector services should first be checked out to see if they can be dealt with by means of "civil society" initiatives; in other words, by appealing to the duty of subsidiarity incumbent on all citizens.

RUNNING A BUSINESS IS BECOMING MORE DIFFICULT

The change from a national to a European market and then to the global market of today has meant that entrepreneurs have had to completely revise their goals and their methods of working. The amount of knowledge required has grown enormously, and is continuing to grow at an ever faster pace! Given the increasing complexity of the tasks involved, the authoritarian management style traditionally adopted by entrepreneurs has had its day.

True, the management style in medium-size enterprises is in many cases still reminiscent of the days when the entrepreneur was very definitely "the boss." But that, too, will change as the responsibilities of leadership become ever more onerous and difficult. For it is becoming increasingly hard both to deliver success and to retain family control by insisting on running a business simply by virtue of the fact that one owns it. It is already becoming clear that soon it will no longer be ownership that entitles someone to head up a business, but proven competence alone. An epoch-making cultural shift, indeed!

In the previous century efforts were made to enhance the productive capacity of the man at the top by introducing new management aids and techniques. I would point here to developments in communication technology and intracompany information systems, and also to the important device of delegating responsibility to large numbers of other people. But even these measures are no longer sufficient in view of the rapidly increasing difficulties of running a business. Economies across the entire globe, therefore, face the same question: Given the changed perception of themselves that people have within the world of work, is it not imperative that we attempt a fresh approach to management methodology?

Over the last couple of centuries there have been many new initiatives in this direction, each intended to complement the others, such as the efforts to provide a comprehensive social safety net and to achieve greater fairness in material terms. The relevant exertions on the part of politicians and the various associations formed by those responsible for wage negotiations are characteristic of this process. Legislation on these matters was based on the assumption that trust and cooperation would prevail, but the tariff partners opted instead for a culture of conflict. There has been some progress—but it certainly cannot be said that the conflict has been resolved at the institutional level. The losses caused by industrial disputes under the current system—which have a considerable social impact—are much too high, and constitute a dangerous obstacle to the international competitiveness that is nowadays required.

If we don't hit on a better solution to this problem, the next generation faces the threat of a slow but steady decline in its standard of living, and correspondingly dramatic arguments about how to stop the rot.

People's present-day perception of themselves require that society be so ordered as to meet the following criteria:

- it must offer opportunities for self-fulfillment;
- it must be fairer;
- it must encourage solidarity wherever subsidiarity proves impossible;
- it must provide security and continuity;
- it must be progressive by its very nature.

When considering these criteria it is worth pondering why our society has never succeeded during the whole course of its history in creating conditions of this kind, for the mistakes of the past might serve as a useful lesson to us as we try to formulate a new social order. In seeking to throw light on these matters, we have to take note of the fact that the multifariousness and imperfection of human nature have always made it extremely difficult to arrive at the requisite consensus. These, I would suggest, are some of the traits that have gotten in the way of such a consensus:

- egotism and egocentricity;
- limited powers of insight;
- dissension concerning the issue of fairness;
- an inability to meet one's obligations to society;
- dishonesty;
- vanity and a thirst for power.

In casting around for a system that is fair to people we should also consider the solutions arrived at by other cultures and ask ourselves whether they can't perhaps offer us some useful tips both for now and for the future. I am thinking here particularly of the following:

- the stability of Chinese cultures;
- the ability of Roman law to engender good order;
- the development of democracy in Greece;
- the Christian conception of mankind;
- the efforts today to establish norms that are international and humane.

In seeking to draw up a new social and economic order we should be careful not to replace old dogmas with new ones, simply because we don't know any better. To be better than the old, any new order of things must be in accord with the way we now perceive ourselves by being truly humane—and by carrying the day with regard to the defects highlighted earlier, and by proving its humane credentials over time. It must also be able to go the distance in the competition between different systems! As is clear from my own experience, and also from the results of the Bertelsmann Foundation's analysis of various socially relevant strategies,

what is needed in order to achieve all this is a pluralistically organized, international approach, and a set of criteria designed to measure results. Aims, methods, and outcomes must all be compared
and evaluated.

In making this proposition I am taking it on trust that the ethical standards of the world's different cultures are in many respects
capable of being harmonized with one another. The misery and
danger besetting the world today are so very plain, it seems to me,
that peoples and their governments will be persuaded to make the
necessary compromises.

ENTERPRISE CULTURE AS AN ANSWER
TO GLOBAL COMPETITION

This book has already dealt on several occasions with the premises
of enterprise culture, and with the way it operates. What we need
to do at this stage is to address the question of whether Germany
can improve its competitiveness by actually applying the enterprise culture system. Various problem areas will be looked at in
this context, as follows:

Given the way people generally perceive themselves today,
most employees do not want to be mere functionaries obediently
doing their duty: in their working lives as much as in their private
lives, they want to be properly involved and make their own creative contribution. However, no such willingness to identify with
the job can emerge in an environment characterized by conflict and
standoffs between capital and labor. We should therefore realize
that we can now replace the attitudes currently prevalent in the
world of work with the constructive energies of a motivation-based
identification with the aims and methods of enterprise culture! The

prerequisites for such a change are already in place. Enterprise culture is fully tried and tested!

Similarly, other criteria, too, point to motivation and identification as being the essential basis of work in an enterprise culture. I would cite the following indicators:

- commitment;
- creativity;
- attentiveness to quality;
- flexibility;
- low absenteeism;
- changing patterns in the labor market.

We may thus draw the following conclusions:

1. With all due respect to the merits of the "tariff partners," we have to ask whether the present goals of capital and labor are in tune with circumstances today, given that people now perceive themselves in new ways.

2. As in the case of public sector working methods, the authorities are being very slow to reappraise and revise the scope for action ceded to unions and employers by the state. Roman Herzog, the former Federal President, has spoken in this context of the "sluggish pace of reform."

3. Comparing relevant economic data with those of other countries can also show us very rapidly why Germany—with its outdated ways of doing things—is not achieving the progress it is potentially capable of.

It is not difficult to see the political consequences of these mistaken policies. Before long the standard election-time promises of "jam tomorrow" will not be enough to reassure the voters. People have a right in this day and age to expect improvements in their standard of living. There must accordingly be a public debate as to whether there aren't better ideas and better ways of doing things. Is it really necessary for public opinion to evolve in such a dilatory fashion, or is it possible for us to become proactive ourselves both as citizens and as businessmen and lead the way through our own example?

In my own long career as an entrepreneur I have sorted out problems enough and thereby found proof abundant that as committed democrats we can indeed make things happen in a civil society. In this respect enterprise culture has proved itself particularly well, both in human terms and at the economic level, and I am delighted that the principles of this new order of things within the world of work have caught on not only in Germany but also abroad. People have at last come to appreciate that we embrace new aims and methods in order to ensure that in the world of work, just as much as anywhere else, people can realize their full potential as human beings and attain a real sense of personal satisfaction.

Our culture rests essentially on our own regional and national experience; but since global rules will tend to prevail in future, we will need to find new aims, new methods, and new standards. This process must not be forced through in a hurry: it must come about gradually on the basis of people's experience of the different circumstances that life now brings. The new pressures and habits that this involves will ultimately yield a new culture. And the more that people understand their new circumstances and respond to the pressures they entail, the more effective and humane the learning process will be. To judge by all the lessons of history, this can probably only be accomplished over a long period of time, but the process should nonetheless be speeded up if possible. We must try to combine the development of worldwide solutions with bold progressiveness, but also with patience and tolerance. What will ultimately prove decisive, however, is not the rapidity of the learning process, but our success—or otherwise—in attuning the new norms to the essential nature of mankind. Rather than fight this process of change, people should confront the challenge posed by progress and its attendant pressures, and be willing to try new ways of doing things within the framework of a workable and humane world culture. Mankind has never yet faced a challenge of this scale!

If we now—while bearing in mind our own cultural traditions—reflect on what the desirable goals of a global community might be, we should take account of the following considerations:

1. All systems must have the nature of mankind as their essential guiding principle.

2. No system may claim sole or ultimate validity. A capacity for change and a readiness to learn will increasingly be the basis for stability within the human community.

3. The desire for progress is understandable and justifiable, particularly in this era in which we now live! A democratic form of society can create the conditions for progress far more effectively than any hierarchical system.

4. For progress to be achieved, freedom, creativity, and courage are just as indispensable as the principle of competition. More creatively minded people must now be called upon to assume responsibility for implementing the new goals and new arrangements.

5. Within an overall framework dedicated to humane values, there must be an insistence on efficiency and fairness, and also on solidarity and subsidiarity.

6. The major organizations that have come into being during this present era—such as those of the state—must no longer be centralistically and hierarchically structured. Decentralization, transparency, measurability, and competition, as well as staffers identification with their jobs, are all essential prerequisites if such organizations are to be run effectively.

7. The stability of a culture rests not least on there being a consensus in respect to both forms and values. The global development of such cultural components takes time, patience, and tolerance. New rules must be tried out, and the educational system must teach ethical values and the basics of involvement just as intensively as it does professional expertise or craft skills. The private sector is particularly well qualified to develop these new "rules of the game" given the unique experience it has accumulated through the pressures of competition—and it has already proved that many different cultures are keen to benefit from economic cooperation. This is an exemplary development that should be taken much further! It will soon lead to greater understanding and to a cooperative spirit.

The right way to proceed, in my view, is to set about the necessary changes one by one. Each stage of the readjustment must be backed up by full acceptance of the various efforts that have preceded it. The harmonization of global cooperation must also be undertaken very carefully. Confidence can be built up by working together in the fields of culture, trade, and travel, and this also establishes modes of cooperation that will later prove valuable in more difficult areas of activity, such as that of political interaction. Economic cooperation is welcomed by almost all peoples and cultures, since it brings the promise of social progress and a better standard of living. This hope is an altogether realistic one, and at the same time it helps people to learn to act for the benefit of their communities. I have no doubt that proceeding in this step-by-step way will enable even difficult issues to be dealt with peacefully—matters such as human rights, religious tolerance, or the mutual accommodation of conflicting political dogmas.

One example of these pressures forcing us to learn new habits is the vexed question of who is really in charge in the private sector—a persistent bone of contention among the unions, employers, and political parties! The conflict over this issue has now been going on for some two hundred years. But I hope that the business culture system and greater transparency as to the facts will enable us to resolve this complicated conflict. Given the way that people perceive themselves today, we need "rules of the game" that are humane and fully in tune with the nature of society. And enterprise culture is rooted in precisely these principles! My thesis is this: In future it will no longer be ownership or the power of the capital market that determines management strategy, but a regime chosen for its managerial expertise. The path to success and competitiveness will not be revealed to us by the culture of conflict, but by efficiency and a spirit of cooperation! Only those who measure up to these criteria should be given the opportunity for advancement. Up to now there have been few such people—but in future there must be many, given the increased difficulty of the job and the need for larger numbers of managers.

We can consider it a tremendous stroke of good fortune that plenty of suitable people are already available to meet this need! For the inevitable management implications of a systematic delegation of responsibility have meant that more people with managerial experience are now available, just as we supposed would be the case. Managerial skills are not only a matter of having the necessary talent; they can be nurtured and enhanced through experience. These developments will not only represent a challenge for our educational system, they will also put a premium on experience and on-the-job learning.

In my long career in business management I was lucky enough to be able to grasp these propositions and put them to the test. There are very sound reasons why even top figures in politics, the organs of state, and the economy—both at home and abroad—are pinning their hopes on the new system that is "business culture." What we are doing, after all, is reconfiguring the world of work in a more humane way, and opening up a vast reservoir of human creative energy!

7

PREREQUISITES FOR DECENTRALIZED MANAGEMENT IN THE STATE SECTOR

A RETURN TO THE ORIGINAL IDEA OF DEMOCRACY

In former times, a ruler's power position—which in most cases depended essentially on brute force—was manifest in his actions and their consequences, but not in any form of plausible legitimacy. Their "subjects" were expected to be grateful if their lives were at least bearable. Ruling elites have certainly stuck up for their subjects on occasion, but doubtless always as a kind of afterthought.

The notion of democratic participation in the evolution of political attitudes, which first emerged in Greece, came about because the community was under permanent military threat from external powers. The independence of thought that characterizes Greek philosophy meant that nonsensical authoritarian decisions were rejected in favor of sensible ones arrived at through dialogue. The battle between different opinions took place in the agora, in the presence of everyone. The speakers were known to all, as were their competence and credibility. This way of exchanging opinions enabled both the audience and the speakers to acquire a deeper awareness of the problems at issue. The resulting decisions were thus more conducive to greater stability within the community as a whole.

Little remains in our present-day democracy of the conditions that enabled the Greek system to work so well. The politicians competing with one another for power are generally known to people only via the media, and in stating their case they are often long on rhetoric but short on substance. Furthermore, the political issues involved are so complex today that the man in the street can scarcely follow the argument.

Another problem lies in the fact that the media are in a position to manipulate public opinion to a dangerous degree. It is thus possible these days for voters to be long deceived as to the consequences of questionable decisions. This means there is little transparency with respect to political aims and outcomes. Decades of ideological polemics have made it very difficult for voters to understand what really lies behind the developments that take place in their society. The resulting diminution of interest in political issues and institutions has further intensified people's loss of any clear sense of direction.

MINIMUM STATE INTERFERENCE—BUT MORE INVOLVEMENT ON THE PART OF CITIZENS!

The oppressive authoritarianism of the political and religious regimes that prevailed in Europe in earlier centuries caused a constant stream of emigration to the United States, where the newcomers, mindful of their bad experiences under European despotism, adopted the motto "minimum state interference!" To ensure that the various functions necessary for the good order of a society were indeed carried out, people in America made themselves available for public service roles on a quite astonishing scale, and thus a citizenry arose that was fully involved and always ready to take responsibilities upon itself. This kind of involvement still plays a remarkable democratic role in modern America's political and economic spheres of activity!

An expansion of the state's administrative apparatus occurred only later, once the scale and complexity of public services began to increase significantly. Even then, however, people's abiding sense of how a civil society operates meant that they were far more effective than Europeans in challenging rules and regulations as to their aptness and efficiency. For any innovation to be deemed right and proper in Europe, it was only necessary to show that it conformed with approved procedures. This amounted in effect to a disastrous insistence on obedience and stasis!

The level of citizens' satisfaction with their social order is thus quite rightly much higher in America than in the European Union. That the low esteem in which the state is held here also extends to its individual representatives is demonstrated with particular clarity at election time in the assessments of leading politicians voiced by the media and by the voters. The citizens of Germany have lost their trust in politics.

A SHIFT IN OUR AIMS: PUTTING SUBSIDIARITY ON A PAR WITH SOLIDARITY!

Although subsidiarity is a constituent element of the democratic system, German politicians rarely demand it of their citizens, as it is scarcely the way to win votes. This has led to the widespread misconception that the state's essential role is to provide assistance, and to promise yet more benefits at election time. Whereas citizens in the democracies of the English-speaking world gladly take responsibilities on themselves and want minimal state interference. German voters have grown used to the idea that all society's shortcomings have to be sorted out by the state.

Here, too, people complain about inefficiencies in the public domain and about the heavy burden of taxation—but it clearly occurs to almost no one to ease the state's task through their own personal involvement. This is perhaps primarily because the politicians themselves have failed to press the right buttons. Our politicians should therefore point more often to the example of America's civil society, which enables government expenditure to be kept at 30 percent of gross national product, whereas in Germany it amounts to a hefty 45 percent! Far from presenting arguments based on this alarming differential, however, people in the lower ranks of our political parties are currently advocating an *increase* in government expenditure! And when they fail to make headway with these proposals because tax levels are already so high, they will try to achieve the same goal by raising the national debt. How fortunate we are that the European Commission has shut the door on such practices!

In view of these widespread political failings it is high time that we engage in a fundamental debate in Germany about the philosophy and function of our democracy! True, a democratic state exists for its citizens—but it is a grave error for our politicians not to counter the general impression that by paying their taxes people have done enough for society. Given the sheer scale of the demand for services assailing the political parties and the state, as well as the political nature of many laws and regulations, it is essential that more citizens commit themselves to doing whatever they can for the state. Without an active civil society, the state becomes the plaything of its bureaucratic institutions, which are often less concerned with making political progress than with consolidating their own rights and privileges.

The call for subsidiarity in our democracy means that each and every citizen and private institution must do everything in their power to help themselves before they seek assistance from the state. It is the duty of our politicians to convey this fundamental requirement of any democratic system to the voters, and to call on them to volunteer their services on a larger scale. It may well be easier to convey these truths within our democratic community if we use examples from the past to demonstrate that solidarity and humane values can only prevail if people are also prepared to embrace subsidiarity.

THE EFFECTS OF EFFICIENCY AND TRANSPARENCY IN THE PUBLIC SECTOR

Over the last hundred years we have become accustomed to an economic order governed to a considerable extent by *competition* and its necessary concomitant, *efficiency*. In accordance with this, monopolies and cartels are nowadays banned by law. The idea of a free market economy is taking hold even in developing countries, who for want of private sector alternatives initially tried state capitalism.

This makes it all the more astonishing that many leading politicians in Germany still believe that different rules apply to the state. In education, health, and social services, of all places, they seem almost incapable of imagining that performance standards, efficiency, and progress could be of any relevance. It is time we grasped the simple fact that state monopolies, too, are out of date in a period of change, and can lead to a grotesque failure to revise goals and apply resources appropriately—as is drastically apparent at the present time. In most areas of state activity a lot more could be achieved with less money.

In a century in which competition and change are determining the pace of developments, the interests of social progress require that new rules be developed and tested for all state activities, and our political leaders must regard this not as an option but as an imperative. Why should a system not prove its worth in the public sector when it has already proved successful in the private sector, and is standard practice in other countries?

On the basis of the trials that I and my colleagues in the Bertelsmann Foundation have been running for decades on behalf of the public sector, I can today confirm without reservation that competition produces exactly the same beneficial effects in the public sector as it does in the private sector. If those in authority had sufficient courage and a better understanding of the processes involved here, it would be possible to make astonishing progress quite quickly in the various politically critical areas. We would then not only have sufficient financial resources; before long we would also have managers capable of taking charge of a public sector fully geared to efficiency and competition. The vexed issue of "performance-related pay," which at present seems completely intractable so far as the state and politics are concerned, would then be viewed by voters in a different light, for our citizens are entirely sympathetic to the notion that if someone performs well, they should be paid well.

It is particularly important in a democracy, therefore, that everyone should be able to find out how things stand within the state sector as regards efficiency. The fact that we in Germany still idly put up with the habits and the jealously guarded rights and privileges of the past is, in my view, irresponsible. The leaders of hierarchical systems often have good reason to conceal what they really want and what they are really up to. A democracy, on the other hand, has an obligation to its citizens to be open and transparent with respect to its aims and conduct. Are we already back on the road to a hierarchical society?

What we lack in the political domain is the relentless pressure to reform that comes from competition, and which is so familiar to us from the private sector. And this pressure is not so much needed in the lower echelons or in terms of working methods, it is needed above all at the senior leadership level. Businesses have every reason to invest far more effort, time, and money in the quality of their top leaders. This investment is complemented by regular and detailed assessments of each individual's performance. Examples from the past should teach us that progress and continuity of management are part of the lifeblood of any major organization. Our democracy is not rendered legitimate simply by virtue of the fact that it is humane in concept; to carry conviction it must also be efficient and competitive!

In developing my argument I have thus far drawn attention only to those particular energizing effects that have been generally exploited in trade and industry. If the new enterprise culture system were also to be applied in the public sector, however, further positive effects could be achieved in addition, as follows:

1. If the project of a major delegation of responsibility to lower levels were to be enthusiastically implemented, the present shortage of creative thinking would very largely be overcome. By introducing performance incentives—just as tenable a proposition in the state sector as in the private—many managers and other staff can be induced to change their ways once defects have been identified in the way things are organized or dealt with.

2. At present, however, changing the rules is a laborious process. If the state were to redefine its aim as "progress" in place of "doing everything by the book," we wouldn't need to worry much longer about the sluggish pace of reform in Germany! What is called for is *more* courage to make *more* progress!

3. All that would be needed to very quickly reveal and hence eliminate the worst drawbacks of our system is a comparative analysis of all analogous state activities throughout Europe—a process that would be quite easy to undertake these days.

4. In an enterprise culture context, however, one should argue not only in terms of greater efficiency, but also in terms of the potential it offers for people to find satisfaction and meaning in their lives! The present defects in the state and in the political domain have led to a dangerous apathy and have made people deeply weary of politics and politicians. To make progress, we need our citizens to be satisfied with the state and its governance.

5. The enterprise culture system *can* also be applied to the public sector, and without losing any of its effectiveness. If we believe that a more effective democracy is worth striving for, then we must also opt for the best available system for running the public sector—and that system is enterprise culture!

RETAINING CULTURAL INDEPENDENCE
WITHIN A COMMUNITY OF NATIONS

As a kind of staging post on the path to global cooperation we are seeing the emergence of large economic blocs. The European Union is one such example. It is plainly evident here that the requisite degree of international cooperation—sought mainly for economic reasons—is more easily achieved if people are able to retain their own familiar culture to the fullest possible extent.

This is not only understandable but also much to be recommended in a period of rapid change. Given people's limited capacity to learn new ways, we should not make things unnecessarily difficult for them. Making the various different cultures more homogeneous is no doubt desirable, but it is not the most pressing task at present. What we have to do first is to improve people's standard and quality of life! And the best way to achieve that is through economic cooperation. Then, as a necessary result, the various cultures will in time come to resemble each other.

We can clearly see these developments taking place in our own time as the European Union increases in size. Even cultures that seem rather alien to us are keen on economic union because they expect it to bring their citizens a better standard of living and hence give their nation greater stability. The political pressures underlying this phenomenon are easy to understand, and in many cases directly observable.

The process of international integration has to be supported by majority opinion in the countries concerned—this will make it more rapid and more successful! Any attempt to force such a process on areas of the world with hierarchical political systems is fraught with risks and inevitably entails treading a circuitous and highly troublesome political path. That this is the case is already accepted wisdom wherever efficiency is paramount, such as in the private sector or in law enforcement, customs, and intelligence agencies. So far as implementing suitable forms of international cooperation is concerned, it is simply a matter of time before more humane and hence more successful political structures become established. The tragic conflict between Chechnya and Russia, whereby Russia is seeking to put a stop to decentralizing tendencies within its own sphere of influence, clearly demonstrates how very necessary it is to understand and foster the learning process!

CONSEQUENCES FOR THE STATE'S EFFICIENCY AND CHOICE OF GOALS

Given that all jobs are more demanding these days, it is essential that people take active steps to become specialists in their fields of work. Exactly the same considerations apply to the sphere of politics and the state. But because of the lack of competitive pressure, the tendency to inertia remains unacceptably strong in these areas. Our motto today, however, has to be this: Anyone who promises progress must also be prepared to abandon outdated habits. Whereas in the private sector the pressures of competition gave us a very short, sharp lesson on the market value of the status quo, the same lesson is learned in a state system devoid of competition only after very long periods of failure. We must amend our laws and our constitution in such ways as to impose new goals and new working practices on our state apparatus—otherwise it will doubtless remain stuck in the same old rut that it is in today!

To ensure progress and the transformation of our state on competitive and humane lines, the following changes must be put in place:

1. Competition must be introduced into all public services. This can be done immediately. Those affected by the change would rapidly get used to it. Costs could be drastically reduced!

2. In this day and age the state does not by any means need to perform *all* the functions that were originally bestowed on it for the better good of society. We should honor and gratefully acknowledge the services that the state has provided in the past, while also pointing out that, thanks to the pressures of competition, private initiatives now yield better results in terms of quality, efficiency, and the capacity for continuing development. The state must be compelled by law to reduce the number and extent of the jobs that it does to an absolute minimum!

3. Transferring tasks from the state to its citizens is another important element in the modernization of our democratic system. It isn't simply a matter here of saving costs; above all, it is a matter of making social processes more modern and more flexible through recourse to a civil society.

4. It could lead to a real and enduring improvement in our democratic system if in due course our politicians were able to report that as a result of decentralization the drain on public funds had been reduced.

MAKING PROVEN PROFICIENCY A PRECONDITION
FOR THE NOMINATION FOR ELECTIVE OFFICE

In order to guarantee the quality of service provided to the public, license to carry out professions involving any degree of responsibility is almost always dependent on the possession of qualifications based on rigorous professional examinations, as is the case in medicine, for instance, but also in the skilled trades, where it is almost invariably necessary to pass demanding exams in order to qualify as a master craftsman. In the state sector, too, Certificates of Competence have been introduced for many career pathways in government offices and public service organizations. This practice has also been followed whenever new career paths have been proposed and approved anywhere in the state sector.

This was not always the case. In former times, whoever seized power could also make the rules, and this sometimes produced dubious results, and doubtless *didn't* produce the order and stability that people hoped to see. This makes it rather surprising that even today candidates put forward for election by the various parties are not required to have any form of relevant professional qualification. This is alarmingly reminiscent of the questionable credentials of those former rulers who came to power simply by means of brute force! The argument that candidates nominated by the parties have already sufficiently proved their credentials through their efficiency and popularity offers no substantive evidence of their qualification for office!

The fact that it was possible in China for dynasties to last for two thousand years was to some extent due to the unchanging conditions in which people lived—but the crucial factor was that candidates for the post of regional governor had to prove their competence by passing a special state examination. Given our own unsophisticated approach to leadership matters in both politics and the public service today, it is difficult to imagine that we choose our top people in a truly effective way.

A rule that applies to all major organizations in the world today is that potential leaders must be carefully chosen and carefully schooled. This applies to the military, to the economy, and to the churches in equal measure—and it must also be given serious consideration when it comes to training the political leaders of the future! In a democracy the approval of voters must not rest solely on the popularity of a politician, for politics is a difficult trade involving great responsibility! If it is true for the economy that the key determinant of success is quality of management, then we can safely say that our system of democracy still has a great deal of catching up to do.

A NEW CAREER PROFILE FOR POLITICIANS

It would need to be worked out in detail which particular skills should be included in a training program for politicians—but I shall not dwell on this here. There are plenty of examples of other career profiles that include a suitable array of topics in their training regimen. One matter I *would* like to stress, however, is the importance of an appropriate level of remuneration. Politics should offer much stronger incentives in order to attract highly talented entrants. This must form part of the new career profile that needs to be created for politics, presenting it in the clearest and most attractive light.

Just how important this is in ensuring that a profession attracts new entrants may be clearly observed at present in the health system, much of which is run by the state. In order to drive costs down, the government has kept doctors' salaries and fees at the lowest possible level. Within a relatively short period this has led not only to a quite unjustifiably heavy burden on doctors, but also to a reduction in the number of students entering medicine, which is simply unacceptable in terms of health policy and planning. We are already familiar with developments of this sort in the state-run health service in Britain—yet for some incomprehensible reason no one in this country has drawn the obvious conclusions. If we want an efficient health service, then decisions of this kind are simply irresponsible. What is plainly evident here is a level of naïveté and managerial incompetence that has absolutely no place in a modern democracy!

With respect to developing a new career profile for the politicians of the future, this means (a) reacting in good time to personnel deficiencies, and (b) offering comparable salaries when competing with other professions for well-qualified college graduates. Given this total failure to run things properly, it seems to me only right to propose that the task of developing a new career profile for politicians be entrusted to experts from the private sector and the universities, rather than based on advice from politicians. A similarly characteristic and lamentable dearth of talent among the younger generation of politicians becomes evident after elections when suitable candidates have to be nominated for parliamentary committees and the like. Many people do indeed put themselves forward for office on these occasions—but they tend to be people who are driven by ambition and vanity, whereas candidates of proven competence are shamefully scarce!

It is no good trying to excuse failings such as these by claiming that they stem from a particularly thrifty approach to economic management on the part of the state. That would be a completely misleading explanation. Rather, this whole miserable state of affairs has come about because the state has paid insufficient heed to the principle of efficiency-orientation. All experience in the private sector proves beyond all doubt that cheap managers are very expensive in terms of the poor results they achieve, whereas highly paid entrepreneurial talents are generally a very good value for the money.

To conclude this particular line of thought I should like to offer a prognosis for the future. The state, with its antiquated devotion to "doing everything by the book," is increasingly incapable of keeping pace with the sheer efficiency of a free economy: Its very constitution as prescribed by law condemns it to be a loser!

DEMOCRACY MUST ENSURE TRANSPARENCY

Like all other organizational systems, democracy is not a cast-iron dogma, but a flexible social system that must be adapted to prevailing needs and to the particular way in which its citizens choose to perceive themselves. The goal of "doing everything by the book" that was formulated in the distant past no doubt contributed to social progress at the time—but today it hinders progressive developments that would benefit our citizens!

In a democracy the public should be fully apprised of efficiency levels through an appropriate information system. If performance ratings in the political and public service sectors were to be regularly publicized in the form of international or regional comparisons, it would be possible to put much-better-qualified and more efficiency-oriented personnel into the organizations responsible. The political parties, too, would once again take much more account of the will of the people, and this would in turn make it easier for them to adjust their policies at election time. If we were to follow this path, we would quite quickly find our way back to a position where the state's business was being directed with skill and efficiency—a position that would accord with the fundamental premises of democracy.

Achieving transparency requires an information system along the lines of those that have existed in major companies in the private sector for a long time now. All important areas must be covered so that the public can see quickly and clearly where things are heading. Politicians of note always used to emphasize that democracy is a time-consuming business but leads to the best results! A modern information system, transparency with respect to both plans and outcomes, and effective assessment of developments in the media could easily lead to surprising improvements in political decision making and render our democracy much more flexible.

8

THE SOCIAL RESPONSIBILITY OF THE ENTREPRENEUR IN A DEMOCRACY

THE PARAMOUNT GOAL OF ANY COMPANY: MAKING ITS CONTRIBUTION TO SOCIETY

The issues of fairness, efficiency, and solidarity have been much thought about over the last two centuries, and this has resulted in a very wide variety of goals within the private sector. The concept of ownership was useful as an incentive, but later proved problematic once shares gave their holders a say in running a business.

Private ownership of the capital generated by a business did indeed enable people to accumulate the large amounts of capital that were necessary—but by no means guaranteed their managerial competence or ensured the continuity of the company. During this period liberal capitalism imposed such severe and inhuman conditions on employees that there was repeated industrial strife, and as a result new systems emerged that sought to be fairer and more humane.

Various attempts were made to use socialist or state-capitalist means to ensure compatibility between private capital on the one hand and attentiveness to social need on the other. The crucial prerequisite for progress and competitiveness is the ability to hold one's own in a market economy, and this ability was perfectly exemplified in the successful synthesis that was Germany's social market economy, which enabled the country to achieve remarkable economic success and meet all the market's demands.

The new demands on the economy were the result of tougher competition and the emergence of goals that differed from those of shareholders. It became increasingly apparent that, because of the conflict culture adopted by democratic countries and energetically practiced by the tariff partners, the right of capital to call the shots could be asserted only at the cost of enormous damage as a result of industrial unrest. The challenge that then emerged was to find an economic concept that sought to *harmonize* the interests of capital, management, and labor, and that placed value not on compulsion and discipline but on identification with the job and with the company. Was there any chance that harmonization of the key elements in a company would reduce losses caused by industrial unrest, improve performance, and lead to ever greater success for the company?

To the surprise of experts in economic policy, the enterprise culture concept proved highly successful, and superior to traditional systems with respect to commitment levels, quality, flexibility, and efficiency. The fact that company goals are explicitly geared to the interests of society means that neither state nor company needs to adjust its goals, and saves both from behaving in ways that could be disadvantageous to society and to the economy. Within this new enterprise culture the interests of capital, management, and labor are coordinated by the Executive Board in the way that appears most appropriate and most conducive to the company's success. The joint participation of the different interest groups on the Supervisory Board not only reduces losses through industrial action but also and above all leads to greater commitment and a stronger sense of identification with the company. At the same time it also fosters the kind of attitude within the company that makes it possible to delegate responsibility—an indispensable process today. I would add that it comes as no surprise to me that this system is increasingly catching on not only in Germany but in other countries, too.

TAKING ACCOUNT OF THE GOALS OF CAPITAL, MANAGEMENT, AND LABOR

The method of balancing out the interests of capital and labor within the context of free collective bargaining is of dubious value these days. For it is not superior arguments regarding the economic or managerial merits of the case that win the day in these negotiations, but the superior economic might of one side or the other.

The political parties occasionally attempt to calm things down by seeking to exert a moderating influence on those involved in the negotiations—but the results of such efforts are inevitably colored by the political orientation of whoever is doing the mediating, and are of dubious value to the tariff partners in their fight to achieve their respective aims. These issues have been more intelligently dealt with in other countries, such as Holland, where every effort is made through the "Labor Foundation" to put wage disputes on a more objective footing *before* formal negotiations by setting up a committee of experts appointed by both sides. The Swiss model, whereby decisions on important issues are dealt with at company level has also proved its worth, and has turned out to be superior to our method of settling things through industry-wide wage agreements.

Bertelsmann's tried-and-tested version of enterprise culture adopted numerous features of these approaches, but added to them by also including the interests of shareholders and the opinions of management. The assumption is that the company's management has particular interests in wanting the company to develop successfully and must be able to voice them. Management is the principal factor determining the success of a business, and as a general rule managers are better informed about company matters than shareholders' representatives. Management should therefore assume the additional task of mediating between the interests of capital and labor within the parameters of the company's mission, and in so doing should by no means heed only the interests of shareholders, but should also stick up for the company's goals vis-à-vis shareholders' representatives—one such goal being to take full account of suggestions made by workers and managers when that is of benefit to the company. This is a job that can often be better done by senior management than by the legally prescribed institutions of the Supervisory Board and Works Committee. It should be added here that this procedure by no means flouts the rights of ownership enshrined in Federal German law—indeed, if anything, it is even more faithful to them. The culture conflict principle as manifested in our economy today is under the microscope! We are confronted by a serious flaw in the system!

These various reflections on management technique are grounded in my direct experience of the fact that people's self-perceptions have changed quite radically, and in my firm belief that where it hasn't yet changed it undoubtedly will! People will no longer slavishly and unquestioningly follow rules laid down by their superiors in a hierarchical system; they want instead to bring their own personalities and professional experience into the equation, they want their ideas and their advice to count! By these means it is possible to get everyone involved in a company to identify with its aims, and this is ample justification for the Executive Board to encourage a mutual accommodation of the interests of capital, management, and labor—which in turn paves the way for a large-scale delegation of responsibility.

On the basis of decades of personal experience I can assure those in the various disparate camps who think they know better or who are disposed to preserve the status quo that I have been both surprised and extremely satisfied by the success of my work in this area! Thanks to this new concept we managed to rescue Bertelsmann from its parlous state in a ruined country, rebuild it, then expand it on a barely imaginable national and global scale. Voices from the entrepreneurial camp confidently assured me that my concept would soon come to grief—but exactly the opposite has happened. It seems to me that the business world would do well to ponder the reasons for this turn of events—and in so doing they should also take note of the benefits that have accrued on the purely human level to everyone concerned. Better results made it possible to introduce profit sharing, while the stipulation that responsibility be delegated on a large scale offered unwonted professional opportunities to large numbers of people. The requirement that the management of the entire enterprise be conducted in a spirit of partnership made for much greater mutual understanding and fostered a sense of community. The fact that it is the declared and overriding aim of the company to benefit society enables even those of a critical disposition to identify with the company, as is clear from our regular staff surveys. Needless to say, I am well aware that we still need to make considerable improvements to this system of ours. Nonetheless, as I look back on my professional career I can reasonably say that I am immensely satisfied with the way enterprise culture has turned out. I am grateful to have had the opportunity to make a contribution to social change.

TASKS AND GOALS OF THE REPRESENTATIVES OF THE VARIOUS INTEREST GROUPS WITHIN AN ENTERPRISE CULTURE ENVIRONMENT

1. Tasks and self-perception of the staff

• The staff want to earn their living in the company, and in so doing they expect to participate in its success. They are quite happy with the idea of performance-related pay, and therefore expect to be fairly rewarded for their hard work, for instance, by sharing in the company's profits.

• Staff are well aware that in this day and age both the work process and their own professional expertise need constant updating. They are willing to undertake the necessary training, but in return they expect to be given an opportunity to advise on, or actively participate in, any such reshaping of the work process on the basis of their particular knowledge and skills. They know the responsibility they carry, and fully approve of issues being sorted out within the company through dialogue between the representatives of the various interest groups.

• Voluntary social amenities can overcome difficulties that the state is unable to remedy. The possibilities I should like to mention here are company health plans, pension supplementation, and provision of a social hardship fund. The staff at Bertelsmann is responsible and disciplined in the way they make use of these amenities, which serve to enhance the protection provided by the state.

• The staff's positive attitude regarding the enterprise culture system is an important factor in the working atmosphere within the company and contributes to the flexibility that is so necessary today, in that the staff trusts the decisions made by management and is willing to make any necessary adjustments.

2. The responsibility of management

Management must take an entrepreneurial approach and marshal and coordinate the resources involved in a production process in such a way that it is competitive. An exemplary demeanor, expert knowledge, creativity, and managerial know-how are necessary prerequisites for this. A manager's compensation should be performance related.

3. The Supervisory Board monitors and advises the Executive Board. Its members are under an obligation to support the aims of the company and in particular the guiding principles of enterprise culture.

NEW GOALS FOR EMPLOYERS AND UNIONS

If we look at the key elements that employers and unions have had to deal with over the years in their negotiations on wages and working conditions, they boil down to the following issues:

- a decent standard of living;
- performance-related pay;
- opportunities for staff to enhance their skills;
- security of employment;
- legal rights ensuring protection in respect to unemployment, sickness, and old age.

To some extent these issues have been resolved. In the meantime, however, people's self-perceptions have changed as a result of the different conditions in which they now live. This has given rise to new expectations. Thus, for instance, people now expect their jobs to offer plenty of opportunities for self-fulfillment and professional success. On grounds of fairness staff members wish to share in their company's profits. They expect management to ensure job security by taking appropriate steps to safeguard the continuity of the company. In their everyday dealings with their supervisors or line managers they expect to be treated as equal partners.

To date, these new expectations have only been partly met by the tariff partners despite all their efforts. There is still total disagreement about the actual means whereby such expectations might be fulfilled, and also about how any such means should be implemented. So long as the tariff partners fail to understand or to accept the implications that flow from the emergence of new, more modern goals and therefore have no appropriate solutions to offer, bruising disputes are bound to arise as a result of global competition and the increasing demands of the market. Settling these disputes by resorting to strikes does not serve any positive purpose, any more than the whole conflict culture approach does, though it is keenly endorsed by our politicians.

This present discussion can only be resolved if we take stock of the changed conditions in which people now live, and especially the new way in which people perceive themselves. The problem certainly can't be solved through the kind of ruthless pursuit of self-fulfillment that is so common these days, nor through any dogmatic interpretation of economic systems!

A genuine willingness to cooperate and to be part of a team is called for today much more than under the hierarchical systems of old. The premises underlying a consensus of this sort need to be defined, understood, and tested—but our dyed-in-the-wool tariff partners are still far from even beginning to think along such lines. The law of the jungle still prevails here: Whoever is strongest wins. The results achieved in other countries that have tried a cooperative approach have been largely ignored in Germany, and are simply not wanted. On the basis of my wide experience with a great variety of Bertelsmann Foundation projects, I recommend tackling the issue by means of a research project consisting of numerous discrete experiments! I advise people to approach the problem without any prejudices, to keep their eyes open for solutions that are already out there in the world and thus readily available, and then to try things out in a series of experiments at home and abroad in order to establish what works and what doesn't.

I myself would gladly offer help and advice in the event of a dispute about methods. It is not by chance that the consensus model developed by the Bertelsmann company has achieved great success both at home and abroad. We welcome dialogue and believe that we will achieve our goals—not least in social terms—by showing understanding, fairness, and knowledge of human nature, rather than by sticking doggedly to the experiences and attitudes of the previous century.

THE ENTREPRENEUR IN A CIVIL SOCIETY

Democracy exists for the sake of its citizens, but it can only be sustained if its citizens are actively committed to it! The state's need for its citizens to show subsidiarity applies equally to entrepreneurs, and while the latter have every right to decide what particular contribution they wish to make, they do not have the right to stand completely apart from society.

The professional skills of an entrepreneur qualify him to make all manner of valuable contributions to society, which he can offer in his hometown, for instance. He can bring his experience to bear in an extremely telling way on his local town council and its various committees. He can give advice to the town's service providers and distinguish himself by becoming a generous patron of its cultural life. Local trusts and foundations are increasingly being set up these days, and these, too, are ideal things for entrepreneurs to become involved in! Other areas that are especially worthy of an entrepreneur's attention are the education system in its many different manifestations, and also the health system, particularly its "early diagnosis" and "preventive medicine" functions, issues that are just as important within the local community of the town as they are in the entrepreneur's own company. Numerous other examples could be cited, but these will surely suffice.

However, entrepreneurs should not only become involved in such things themselves, they should underline their democracy's need for subsidiarity by encouraging their managers and staff to contribute to society. There is plenty of scope for such things within a company, for instance, by supporting community associations and cultural events. Consideration should also be given to various different opportunities for encouraging community spirit, and in this respect the education of the young deserves special attention.

Entrepreneurs are generally extremely busy, but once they appreciate their own dependence on society they will realize that they, too, have opportunities to help—if not by becoming directly involved, then at least by contributing financially.

I wish that members of society here in Germany, and more particularly the leaders of our economy, would play a more vigorous role in these tasks that are such an important part in a democratic civil society! In other countries senior executives have more opportunity than most to see at firsthand how the burdens on a lean state can be reduced by the active involvement of its citizens. A "civil society" is more humane, more efficient, and better suited to prevailing circumstances!

9

ENSURING CONTINUITY: A SOCIAL RESPONSIBILITY

THE IMPORTANCE OF CONTINUITY IN THE PAST

Over the course of history very different values have been placed on cultural continuity. For thousands of years those in power maintained that unquestioning adherence to law and tradition was their subjects' best means of ensuring bread on the table and peace in the land. In the past the powerful cared little for the notion of progress. Progress seemed to imply a challenge to tradition and was regarded as a danger. Supposedly risky reforms were therefore rejected out of hand. It seems quite striking, in any event, that where stasis prevailed it was precisely the most stable dynasties that were generally incapable of developing their system in a progressive sense, despite the fact that they relied on the great statecraft of their ruling elite.

How very differently we view tradition and continuity today! In the Western world, and increasingly in Asia, the capacity to learn and to progress is regarded as a crucial prerequisite for securing the future, with great importance attached to peaceful competition between different systems. It is no longer rulers who determine developments, but ordinary people, who do so by making countless choices that are open to them as a result of competition. This being so, we need to ask ourselves which elements of our traditional culture—for instance, within the realm of ethical values—should be retained, and which areas require us to develop fresh ideas. It is striking that academics and other researchers have so far come up with little of substance on the question of how best to ensure the necessary continuity. This is all the more astonishing given the fact that in tackling this problem we have the colossal advantage of being able to review and compare the relevant experiences of all other cultures in the world thanks to modern information technology.

THE EMERGENCE OF A NEW CULTURE IN CONDITIONS OF CHANGE

In the past, culture was at the service of the powerful. Those who hold power today are the politicians, who are mandated by the voters to work in their interest.

In a sense, the same holds true in the economic realm: As markets increasingly open up and living standards rise, the choices available to consumers put them in a position to influence the production of goods, as well as their quality and value. Parallel to these consumer-controlled developments, the media also exercise a homogenizing influence on people's cultural attitudes worldwide. We may regret the fact that in the process regional characteristics have diminished in importance; all in all, however, the global-village effect means that different peoples understand one another better, and there is less risk of military conflict. As a result of this new way of thinking there is already a perceptible effort across the whole world to achieve dialogue, cooperation, and peace.

In order to develop things even further in this more humane direction, however, we must ensure that the innovatory power of competition is brought to bear in every area of life, and rendered far more effective in the sphere of politics.

1. While fully acknowledging the social importance of the competition principle, we must not lose sight of the fact that ultimately reforms are only justifiable if they benefit people. Without careful and judicious transitional arrangements the negative effects of competition could outweigh its advantages. This problem has become very apparent to us in the context of public health policy decisions and the management of the labor market, as well as in the context of the World Trade Organization's efforts to liberalize markets.

2. The authoritarian state was a product of historical circumstance. It failed for the very good reason that it was incapable of providing the kind of leadership that is called for today. People reveled in their new perceptions of themselves and in the great opportunities for individual freedom that came with them, but paid insufficient heed to the concomitant obligation to contribute to the life of their communities. After the Second World War our educational institutions were hesitant to convey to their charges the importance of responsibility and community spirit. In the past there was excessive emphasis on "the community" relative to the rights and duties of individuals, and one can still detect a residual fear of this in our educational system.

3. We may well regret the fact that the home—the key educational influence in a child's life—no longer does enough to correct

inappropriate behavior, but we also need to appreciate the fact that it is difficult in a libertarian age to teach people how to behave. After the various wrong turnings that the education system has taken in recent decades, it is therefore all the more encouraging to see that young people are once again prepared to become involved, to shoulder responsibility, and to acknowledge that our society must be efficiency oriented.

During the current process of change it will prove especially necessary—though also time-consuming—to impart ethical values and a sound perspective. The churches and the state have unfortunately done too little to help young people in this respect. Thus, while they appreciate that they must respect the law, the liberalizing tendencies they see at every turn make them think it unnecessary to shape their lives according to ethical values and religious beliefs.

Over a period of several decades, therefore, society increasingly fell short of its obligation to give young people the hold in life that they require. They themselves have meanwhile begun to identify the problem, and are trying to deal with the resultant lack of a meaningful perspective. We shall begin to realize before too long that the principle of freedom is not sufficient to ensure that people are ready and able to play their full part in their community. It therefore falls to the younger generation to come up with the makings of a new ethical perspective—one attuned to the new circumstances now prevailing in people's lives, and firmly based on the principles of democracy, human rights, and the duty incumbent on everyone to demonstrate both solidarity and subsidiarity.

These new attitudes are not taking shape in isolation, however, for they are increasingly subject to the influence of international thinking. But we should no longer regard this as a threat to our own culture, but instead realize that by participating in the international learning process we can avoid making mistakes, and can more rapidly attain the goal of a truly humane order of things. Given the disastrous role that nationalism has played in Germany, it well befits the Germans of today to tackle the challenge of creating a new cultural order in a spirit of openness, willingness to learn, and—not least—humility.

THE CULTURAL REPERCUSSIONS OF GLOBAL COMPETITION

The numerous means of communication that are now available make it possible for the citizens of any country at any time to compare its own standard of living with that of its neighbor. Knowledge of this kind ignites new desires! The simplest way for the poorest countries to share in international prosperity seems to be for them to join a large economic bloc, as exemplified by the efforts of the Eastern European states to gain admission to the European Union. The political regimes in the various neighboring states that are not yet part of the EU can scarcely resist this strong desire for integration, especially given the worldwide process of democratization. We are thus witnessing a cultural upheaval of unprecedented magnitude in the economically backward countries of Europe—triggered by the hopes and aspirations of their own peoples. It has to be said that it is highly doubtful whether the people in the relevant countries—and that includes their governments—have any real inkling of the cultural adjustment problems that this integration process will bring. Thus the people of the German Democratic Republic were promised that re-unification would bring them milk and honey—but no one even hinted at the extent to which their whole pattern of life and work would change in the process.

In the context of political integration, the culture of a country must not be regarded merely as so much local color. Culture is a set of habits of mind and action indispensable to the communal life of those to whom it belongs. Such shared habits make the wheels of everyday life go round and make it much easier for people to relate to one another. Language—to take a conspicuous example of communal culture—demonstrates the importance of shared conventions with particular clarity: Without language people cannot understand each other!

Culture also determines how willing a people are to learn and to work efficiently—traits that are essential if a higher standard of living is to be achieved. Too little account is taken of this in the push for economic integration, and as a result the people involved are often disappointed by the outcome of the integration process. In retrospect their former ways then seem more important to them than economic progress, which can only be achieved through much hard work. The political pressures that arise from people's hopes and aspirations will probably continue to determine the actions of politicians—but in view of the now extremely familiar problems of integration, it would seem to be imperative to approach any future projects of this sort with more candor and more sober realism.

Learning and readjustment processes within a culture generally take one or two generations, although the length of time required also depends on the level of development of the particular country. By means of a systematic analysis of social transformation processes in differently developed countries, the Bertelsmann Foundation has demonstrated beyond all doubt that all the various developmental stages follow a logical and inescapable sequence. None of these stages in the learning process can be skipped, no matter how much the state may attempt to force the issue, or how much money may be thrown at the problem. With regard to the whole gamut of developmental phases that any proposed integration may involve, this means that in some cases the adjustment process can even last for centuries.

As the example of the Commonwealth's development aid program demonstrates, this problem is handled much more effectively by Britain than by the United States. Thus President Clinton, speaking in Davos the in spring of 2000, argued for a rapid acceleration of the learning process and a speedier convergence of the different cultures. But it seems questionable whether this is remotely feasible given the huge differences in development between the various cultures. One only has to look at the way things developed in the former U.S.S.R. After the collapse of the socialist system the United States immediately sent Moscow advice about making the economic reforms that were urgently necessary. Their initiative was well intentioned, but it ignored the inherent and inescapable logic of change, grossly overestimated people's capacity to adjust, and inevitably and very quickly proved a failure.

So what are the consequences of a rushed modernization policy? The countries that are already technologically advanced may possibly be able to sustain the pace. But where the predetermined speed of development is excessive, whole regions will become the problem children of globalization, a situation that will not be changed one jot by any measures that the state might take to shore them up—measures moreover that are extremely costly and very inefficient. In other words: Well-intentioned but hasty reform policies serve only to destabilize a society—and as this is already an established fact, no politician can claim that he couldn't have foreseen the consequences of his actions.

At first glance one might get the reassuring impression that the European integration process is being planned in a sensible manner—but here, too, one can reasonably have one's doubts whether the envisioned time frames really are going to prove sufficient. If not, then politicians must react quickly, before things get to be too much for people in the relevant countries.

The same principle applies when it comes to dealing with reforms that turn out in practice to be flawed: In such cases corrective action must be taken with respect not only to the substance of the reform but also to its timescale. Even a planning estimate of twenty years may prove to be far too short. A strategic plan must take account of all relevant factors that might affect the outcome, and in particular it must take all necessary precautions to protect the interests of the country's citizens. It is perfectly possible in this day and age to make firm predictions about how developments will progress in the private and state sectors, and then to identify at a sufficiently early stage the likely requirements in terms of personnel. That there have been numerous lapses in this regard is clear from the current discussions concerning the shortage of engineers and IT specialists, but also from the complaints voiced about the complete absence of any properly qualified pool of potential leaders in politics and the state. Although the media have repeatedly drawn attention to this appalling state of affairs, nothing is being done to remedy it.

I am well aware that it has never been the practice in democracies to systematically groom potential leaders. But in view of the fact that the task of political leadership is becoming increasingly difficult, it is now time to plan ahead and thus set the course for the future. What happens decades from now will be determined by what we decide today. Are our politicians really so completely preoccupied with their everyday business that they have no time to spend on these profoundly important issues?

In this day and age, growth can no longer be left to chance! It would therefore be extremely helpful if in politics, too, we were able to draw the necessary conclusions from trends that are already clearly recognizable—and draw them in time to take appropriate action. In the private sector this has long been achieved by every well-managed company. Why can't the political parties do it too? We have to structure processes of change in such a way that the inevitable transitional stages are identified at an earlier stage and managed in a more humane fashion. Strategic planning and measures to ensure continuity thus belong among the paramount tasks of political leadership.

ENSURING POLITICAL CONTINUITY

In the past, cultivating tradition and preserving the status quo were regarded as the most appropriate ways of safeguarding the future—but people today have come to realize that the radical changes that have occurred in the whole pattern of their lives must very soon be matched by a complete overhaul of habits, customs, and practices. In the course of history all the various impulses that have driven different cultures have found expression in social systems of one sort or another. Thus, for instance, we are unlikely to have forgotten the difference between a socialist planned economy on the one hand, and a social market economy on the other. In the political as opposed to the economic realm we could draw a similar comparison between the hierarchical systems of old and the

constitutional democracies of today. Understanding the nature of
the change at a sufficiently early juncture would certainly be an
important step in the right direction! Systems intended to serve as
a framework for the functioning of a society must suit both the circumstances of the time *and* the convictions of the people involved.
It follows from this that such systems cannot and must not be immutable! Every age is confronted by different problems and has to
pursue its own particular goals, and social systems must accordingly be organized in such a way that they are capable of learning and adjusting. The direction in which they need to change
may be summed up in two crucial words: "competitiveness" and
"humanity"!

It is much easier to judge whether a culture or any of its constituent systems are on the right track if their outcomes are in a
form that can be measured and evaluated. In the private sector it
is competition that produces such judgments and prompts any corrective action that may be necessary—and it does so with unfor-
giving rigor! In politics, on the other hand, developments don't
follow any standard pattern and are more difficult to assess. What
confronts us is a babel of conflicting opinions that is scarcely intel-
ligible to most citizens, let alone susceptible to evaluation.

The constitution of our state obliges its political leadership to
serve the interests of its citizens, and makes the exercise of political
power subject to their vote. On the face of it this arrangement carries conviction—but in actual practice it does not, since the crucial
influence that the voters are supposed to exercise is routinely
evaded, particularly when it comes to filling key positions. Under
the prevailing circumstances, there is no adequate basis on which
voters can make a proper judgment as to which politician is truly
capable of leadership, or which policies are most likely to achieve

their goals. Furthermore, this lack of knowledge on the voters' part is exploited in a counterproductive manner in that their opinions are manipulated with the help of the media. In this respect even democracy has not succeeded in controlling the mighty in their exercise of power, so that to this very day they themselves determine the limits of their power in a quite unjustifiable manner. In my view this fundamental flaw is also the reason why the democratic system is so averse to learning new things, and above all why it is so plainly incapable of building up a well-qualified leadership elite. If the democratic system has staying power despite its sundry weaknesses, then this is chiefly because most people accept the basic principle that power is meant to be legitimized by the people and exercised for their benefit. This belief is a powerful and seductive one! Despite all the disappointments they encounter in practice, people nonetheless hope and believe that democracy will triumph in the end. This unsatisfactory state of affairs is confirmed whenever polls are carried out on the popularity of different professions: Politicians and union representatives—all of them democratically elected—score the least votes! History should tell us that no organization can last very long if its representatives are not respected by the people. The downfall of hierarchical power structures in the past is proof enough, and should encourage us to mend our ways!

It is worth drawing a comparison here with the collapse of socialism, a collapse determined by the system itself. The basic idea of socialism appealed to people and awakened great hopes. But the attempt at realizing the idea in the form of centralistic states that allowed for no learning processes and no readjustments, and above all entertained a totally unrealistic conception of man, led to the failure of this entire corpus of abstract dogma. What we learn from drawing this comparison is that economic and social systems must be so designed that their outcomes can be measured, and they must be exposed to competition and the corrective forces that competition entails. For in the long run hope is not enough; no system can really last unless it delivers real returns for everyone concerned. Let us hope that politics will in future be characterized to a much greater degree by transparency and measurable outcomes, with the result that our systems will become readily comprehensible and will have the full approval and support of the people!

If with this aspiration in mind we look at the political system now prevailing in the Federal Republic, we cannot avoid noting a number of serious shortcomings with regard to the capacity of our democratic system to learn new things:

1. The scale and difficulty of the task confronting our political leaders cannot be dealt with by centralizing power. To tread this path is to head for certain failure.
2. The very limited delegation of responsibility that is currently practiced in the public sector is nowhere near sufficient.
3. Our present practice with respect to delegation can teach us very little because our dedication to the old principle that everything must be done by the book leaves little scope for trying new ideas.
4. The refusal to introduce competition and, in particular, to make managerial performance subject to evaluation favors the preservation of the status quo and makes it difficult to replace unsuitable managers.
5. In every organization leadership is the key determinant of success. Ensuring continuity of leadership is thus a crucial task for any political party. The current personnel problems in German politics will demonstrate the inadequacy of pre-

vailing arrangements for identifying and nurturing potential leaders.

6. In managerial terms it is inexcusable that the opportunities already available for comparing performance in the public and political sectors are not being used, or—worse—that the results of such comparisons are being withheld from the public. Democracy demands transparency!

7. It is a dire state of affairs that mere eloquence in a politician still carries more weight than proven ability.

To sum up: The pressures for reform that currently exist in the Federal Republic are insufficient. The political programs being offered today are scarcely convincing, and cannot be relied on to produce a system that is humane, efficient, and capable of adaptation.

All Western democracies agree that in the economic sphere they cannot do without the driving and invigorating force of competition. This being so it is remarkable that only very few democratic regimes apply the competition principle in the state and political sectors for which they are responsible. Is this perhaps something to do with the widespread but entirely false assumption that competition between the political parties themselves is sufficient?

In any event, this lack of true competition has a devastating effect on the actual practice of politics. If on the other hand the decisions of politicians were to be properly evaluated and made public, as happens in the private sector as a function of competition and of the legal requirements concerning transparency, then the reforms that have been needed for so long could very soon be in place; the electorate could vote for the best policies and the best-qualified politicians, and it would rapidly become apparent how important it is to run the country in a performance-oriented manner.

Fortunately we are currently seeing the beginnings of an important new venture in this direction in the form of a reshaping of local government—a venture that is impressive in itself, and also bodes well for the modernization of our democratic system as a whole. At this level of political management one encounters numerous fellow citizens who not only have direct personal experience of the dire deficiencies of the prevailing system, but also know how things *ought* to be done. And despite having suffered decades of disappointment, these people are willing to give the benefit of their knowledge to help reform local government. Initial moves in this direction have met with great interest in numerous German towns and cities. The new system is based in essence on various successful attempts to restructure municipal administrations in order to make them competitive and performance driven. On the basis of the knowledge thus gained, the aim now is to make the work of city councils more transparent as well.

I have no doubts whatever about the practical feasibility of this reform project—but its political repercussions are likely to prove fascinating! Once citizens base their judgments on facts and objective evaluations of those facts, rather than on promises and rhetoric, then we shall find within a couple of years that we have a very different kind of democracy! A democratic system will emerge that we can trust once again, and that enables voters to really know what they are voting. Institutionalizing this system will not only lead to better decisions and better-qualified politicians, but will also serve to convince citizens that democracy is truly the best political system. The result would be a more stable society, and a much greater involvement in community responsibilities on the part of citizens. What we see taking shape here is the vision of a lean and efficient state—and once the outcomes envisioned for local politics have fully sunk in, I wouldn't be at all surprised if we didn't start asking ourselves whether similar reforms aren't conceivable in other realms of politics as well. Here, too, there is undoubtedly scope for improving efficiency. But let's take things one step at a time: Let's try first of all to make reforms at the local level!

To emphasize once again what is needed for this project to succeed, I should like to conclude by offering the following suggestions:

1. Involvement in local affairs on the part of citizens with appropriate experience.
2. Patience: To be fully tried and tested, a project of this kind needs a time span of at least five years.
3. The latitude to restructure things in the best possible way, and boldness in trying out new methods.
4. No extra money—but full acceptance of the principle that subsidiarity is an essential element of the democratic system!

THE STATE AS GUARANTOR OF CONTINUITY

A democratic state can function properly only if there is full acceptance of what democracy entails. On the one hand, people today are encouraged by their upbringing and by the circumstances of modern life to expect plenty of freedom to do as they wish; on the other hand, they still need to learn that the state also requires them to do their bit to help. There is still insufficient awareness in this respect in Germany, for the gospel of self-fulfillment, so keenly propagated after the Second World War, was for a long time interpreted more along the lines of the popular slogan *"Ohne mich!"* ("Count me out!"). Only now, after half a century, is this error being remedied through the burgeoning of a civil society. As we move forward along the path to further successful reforms, we need to take account of the following problem areas:

1. Comprehensive welfare

• The apparatus of state supports the government in the implementation of its objectives. One goal is for all citizens to be treated equally. When important areas of state provision were being developed in the nineteenth and twentieth centuries—education or health services, for example—best practice was elevated to the status of mandatory practice and enshrined in binding rules and regulations. This resulted in a good and extensive range of services, and a comprehensive welfare system.

• The practice within the state sector of always sticking to the rules rested not only on strict discipline but also on the professional ethos of the officials themselves. For a long time this philosophy produced satisfactory results in the provision of state services.

• However, the concept presupposed that the general pattern of life remained static. But with increasing knowledge and the emergence of methodical competition, questions soon arose as to the proficiency of the system. And there was another question crying out for an answer at this time: What could be regarded as efficient enough, and as having enough scope for innovation? These considerations were rendered even more pressing by the fact that the laws relating to public servants were inflexible and seemingly set in stone.

2. Competitiveness

The numerous extra services provided for citizens in the previous century were indeed the product of a democratic system—but they were delivered through an apparatus inherited from the hierarchical state of old. Under the new democratic order of things the government saw its function as being to protect, control, and care for its citizens. As a result, every successive election campaign with its battle to attract majority support brought an increase in the number of services provided by the state. In due course this gave rise to a plethora of rules and regulations that overwhelmed the normal processes of politics and led to a state apparatus devoid of flexibility.

Politicians finally decided that the best way to get out of this mess was to privatize some of the state's services and thereby expose them to the innovative influence of competition. This procedure proved acceptable to society, and highly effective in terms of minimizing costs. At that stage of things, on the other hand, the possibility of introducing competition into the inner workings of the state itself was simply unimaginable.

3. Limiting state involvement to the bare minimum

As we well know today from the way management techniques have developed, size and complexity make enormous demands on management and leadership skills. This is particularly evident in the case of the state, since, for historical reasons, performance-oriented management methods have never been applied here. But the problem of size is relevant to other organizations, too. Thus, for instance, we witness time and again the collapse of global market leaders and other monopolies. And the state is itself a monopoly! It would be very helpful to the state in the performance of its tasks if politicians were to grasp these basic realities of management science. The call for a "lean" state is amply justified in our day and age!

The democratic system, and the tendency for politicians of all parties to take little care when spending public money, have resulted in the emptying of Germany's coffers. People are now beginning to wonder whether the state's services and subventions are indeed necessary, and are slowly realizing that politicians should not see it as their role to tout special offers in a self-service emporium. The state should only help those who can't help themselves. Instead of always expecting solidarity, we must learn to assert the principle of subsidiarity. We will be amazed at the amount of time this learning process takes! And our politicians—who will have less money to give away at elections—will have the toughest time of all. The learning process would go more smoothly if politicians did not take the easy way out in financial matters, for instance, by borrowing money. They would then be showing true leadership, and would be all the more successful as a result! The outcomes of political decisions would improve, too, if they were reported in a more transparent way that gave a proper account of their financial consequences. What is needed to boost the trust of our citizens is not fresh government borrowing, but thrift and transparency!

4. The mandate to lead

As already mentioned, a very large proportion of our regulatory codes and protocols derived from a period of relatively high stability and hierarchical government. Rules belonging to that form of government no longer meet the needs of today. They satisfy people with respect neither to the performance nor legitimacy of their leaders. It is therefore time to develop a mode of government that combines competent leadership and democratic principles. This may seem a contradictory pairing, but in fact the two things complement each other. For our citizens are quite prepared to take on responsibilities and to be involved in decision making; indeed they want plenty of scope for such things and seek to play their part in public life. At the same time they expect their leaders to be highly qualified professionals and thoroughly decent human beings. The principle that success is the only thing that really counts will remain just as valid in the future as it is now, but straightaway we need to realize that success will henceforth depend chiefly on the *ability* of those in charge. Our political leaders must therefore *not* be allowed to acquire legitimacy simply by dint of being elected. In future no one must be nominated for election to any political office unless they have first gone through a scrupulous long-term training process and successfully proved their mettle in a position of responsibility.

Leaders selected in this way must then not only perform exceptionally well, but also be paid accordingly! Such a practice would by no means involve the state in extra expenditure. On the contrary, it would make for thrift and efficiency, as a glance at the private sector immediately demonstrates: Top executives earn good money, indeed extremely good money, because their work is the cornerstone of their companies' success and profits.

5. Can the state suffer a continuity problem?

There is a widespread conviction in the Federal Republic that the state will never go under. This is probably true, given the number of functions it currently fulfills—but we may well pay for this by experiencing increasing inefficiency and a declining standard of living!

Ensuring the continuity of the state requires at the very least that it remain internationally competitive. And the same principle applies in politics as in business: Any enterprise with its sights set on the future should never be satisfied with a middle-ranking position, since such a position carries too great a risk of slipping further and ultimately failing. Citizens thus have every right to expect the state to make just as much effort as they do in their ordinary lives. This means that we expect our state to do more than merely survive: We trust that it will exert itself in an exemplary fashion, and through its exertions advance the cause of progress in this country!

CAPACITY FOR CHANGE AS A PREREQUISITE OF ECONOMIC CONTINUITY

In my youth I myself experienced just how important tradition still was in both state and society. The precepts handed down by previous generations were regarded as self-evidently valid and could not be questioned. It was only in the second half of the twentieth century that far-reaching changes in almost all areas of people's lives caused the idea of tradition to lose more and more of its importance.

If the experiences of the past no longer serve us given the radical changes that have occurred across the globe, then we must seek new goals and new paths. This is a task that particularly confronts our political leaders. To this end I advise them to take a good look at the strategy adopted by the private sector in response to globalization! I offer the following propositions:

1. Everyone wants security and a rising standard of living. This ambition is best served by economic cooperation among the various nations. Politicians can count on the fact that increased cooperation will meet with citizens' approval.

2. People are afraid of chaos and the collapse of law and order. They quite rightly fear war as a means of settling arguments. Their

need for security and a better standard of living is so strong that they are prepared to give up some of their cultural traditions in exchange for improving their lot within the framework of international cooperation.

3. It must be admitted that people do not always find it easy to recognize the advantages and disadvantages of cultural adjustment processes. But given goodwill, tolerance, and a sober approach to the issues involved, it is generally possible to convey to people that the upside of international cooperation outweighs the downside.

4. It is particularly important in this context that there be an absolute ban on settling differences by force of arms. The great efforts made by politicians in this direction, and the various agreements that they have arrived at, are an encouraging sign.

5. The media and modern information technology could play an important role in ensuring that the world develops in a peaceful manner. Thanks to the Internet people today can exchange information and communicate with one another without regard to national boundaries. With this, we are already on the road to a global culture.

What are the implications for the economy of reflections such as these? We should have the courage to ask whether the traditional components of our economic system are still appropriate to the age in which we now live. Our future opportunities for controlling events and achieving success will depend on our pursuing the right goals, and doing so along the right kind of path.

Let us also ask ourselves a few questions on this issue:

1. The entrepreneur was a key figure at the start of the Industrial Revolution. Entrepreneurs were able to make money thanks to their creative flair. Today those with capital believe they can make

money without making a creative and entrepreneurial contribution of their own! Which of the two makes the more important contribution to running a business in our present era?

2. Employees used to have to do what they were told and were subject to strict discipline. Why is this no longer sufficient today?

3. Today, as in the past, an owner's right to exercise control is safeguarded by law. How successful is this approach in ensuring the continuity of medium-size companies, for example?

4. Why do the largest companies pay their top executives such high salaries? And why do their shareholders agree to this?

5. Employers, unions, and politicians are proud of their conflict culture. Is this attitude justified by their level of success?

6. Is it conceivable that, in future, entrepreneurial and creative people will also be able to assume a managerial role in the public sector on the basis of their proven managerial ability?

In terms of strategic forward planning, correct responses to the above questions could save much time and trouble. My own answers are as follows:

- In future, motivation will be a more important success factor than capital.
- Capital will retain its function as an instrument, but it will not retain its managerial function, not even where ownership rights are involved.
- In the private sector the pressing task of ensuring continuity will be dealt with more rapidly.
- Our experience of global cooperation will influence all areas of society. Our various systems will come under strong pressure to bring themselves up-to-date. We should see this in an entirely positive light!

BASICS OF MANAGERIAL PRACTICE
TO ENSURE CONTINUITY

Continuity is supposed to benefit society as much as it benefits the individual. But continuity does not mean "more of the same"; it does not mean uncritical acceptance of yesterday's precepts with regard to society and the state! Methods and attitudes that have proved their worth in the past will not necessarily do so in the future. Only if conditions remained totally static could the solutions of the past solve the problems of the future. But since that is highly unlikely in a period of change, we constantly have to ask ourselves what would be a better way of doing things. If we fail to ask ourselves these questions, we run the risk of being elbowed aside by our competitors. The adage "to rest is to rust" is more pertinent than ever!

Breaks in continuity are inevitable when the agenda is to move forward and secure the future. However, we can mitigate the negative consequences of change. Our goal must therefore be to ensure continuity in the midst of progress, and to structure change in a humane manner.

Long-term Planning of Reforms

Because of the pressures of competition, the private sector has had to think harder than any other area of society about how to plan for the future. In the process it has devised useful mechanisms for the long-term planning of all important aspects of a business. Over the last few decades, in particular, major companies have come to understand the need to plan strategically for the future. Time requirements have also been factored in, since these have an important bearing in the age of the Internet.

Therefore, if a company decides that major reforms are necessary in order to make progress, those in charge need to have precise answers to the following questions:

1. Which parts of the company will be affected by the reforms?
2. Are the changes to be carried out in a humane manner?
3. What time frame is necessary and permissible?

The question of whether the requisite changes are to be carried out in a humane manner is not merely a rhetorical one! For the answer determines the degree of consideration given to the interests of the staff. With regard to the time frame, one *could* make one's decision on the basis that "time is money"—but this would seriously restrict the scope for structuring the transition in a humane way. The time frame is thus dependent on the company's attitude to those employees who will be affected by the changes! At the same time one should ask oneself whether it ought not to have been possible to make an earlier start on planning the changeover to the new system! Calculating the time required for the change must be viewed as an optimization process. This task involves not only estimating the direct costs of introducing the new system, but also evaluating the potential loss of trust on the part of employees! Given present-day circumstances in the workplace, it needs to be remembered that commitment, creativity, and quality depend entirely on employees identifying with their company and its way of conducting itself. Anyone who rides roughshod over these fundamental elements of enterprise culture can easily find that they have made a very expensive miscalculation!

It is therefore important for a company to inform its staff in good time about any major reforms, taking particular care to convince them of management's determination to carry out the reform process in a humane manner. Any attempts to pull the wool over their eyes would shatter their trust in management for a very long time; deceit would be a grave managerial error!

Long-term personnel planning is equally important. Even in an age characterized by change and flexibility, employees expect not only a decent wage but also security and the opportunity to improve themselves. The company must bring these understandable concerns into sync with its own interests, by, for example, offering staff constant opportunities for further training. This requires considerable effort and financial investment, but not only are the costs worthwhile in themselves, such measures are vital if the organization is to survive. In this context it is striking that it has recently become the practice in major company mergers to assess the quality of a company's managers and the progress it has made in promulgating enterprise culture. People have realized that these factors are economically important.

Ensuring Continuity of Leadership

One of the key tasks in personnel planning is ensuring that there will be continuity of leadership in the event that the CEO or other senior executives leave the company. This task must be dealt with on a long-term basis with attention not only to practical and professional issues but also to its implications in human terms!

Selecting, trying out, and preparing a successor for the role of CEO should be initiated at least ten years before the changeover takes place, as a very long time is required for suitable candidates to learn the ropes and prove their mettle. This applies particularly to Personnel and Marketing. There must be an annual assessment interview of the potential appointee by those above him, giving him an opportunity to work on any weaknesses he may have. If it becomes apparent at any stage that the proposed succession is not going to work out, steps must be taken at once to find alternative solutions. Extending the period of office of the outgoing CEO should be avoided.

If it becomes evident that a suitable internal candidate is unlikely to materialize, early thought must be given to finding an external candidate, or perhaps even to selling the business. These latter alternatives are particularly appropriate with respect to safeguarding the interests of the staff involved. In the case of a corporation, succession problems should never arise if the company is properly run. If such problems *do* arise, then this indicates serious failure on the part of the Executive Board and the Supervisory Board.

In medium-size businesses the idea of family continuity very understandably looms large. Involving several children in the business in order to try to achieve this is managerially very difficult, however. This course of action is tenable only if there is a clear division of responsibilities, and if the shareholders have unambiguous powers of dismissal. It is almost certainly a better arrangement in the long term to choose just one person to be in charge.

As late as the beginning of the last century it was regarded as highly desirable to seek to maintain family continuity. This goal is very questionable, however, in view of the increasing complexities of running a company, and its increasing capital requirements. It should be borne in mind that only 30 percent of medium-size companies are managed successfully by the second generation of a family, and only 10 percent by the third generation.

On the other hand when heirs inherit a family business their attitude is often characterized by a sense of responsibility to their own firm rather than by any insistence on their right to take direct control. In times of crisis this has proved its worth on many occasions, particularly in the rebuilding of numerous medium-size businesses after the Second World War. But if a family is no longer capable of shouldering the responsibility of running a company in the circumstances of today, it is worth bearing in mind that the heirs, in their capacity as shareholders, can exert a benign influence by ensuring that humane values prevail. Anyone who is brought in from outside to run the company must also take his cue from this consideration.

Even today, therefore, a family can do its bit to facilitate continuity of leadership. The impact of family tradition in terms of continuity and maximization of company performance can thus be regarded as distinctly positive. It is always worth trying to draw on it as much as possible, for humane values and fairness have always formed the basis of any successful community. The family can and must contribute to it!

When heirs inherit family businesses, thought must be given not only to the transfer of executive control but also to the financing problems that this involves. In anticipation of the succession, therefore, a timely decision should be made as to how outside capital is to be raised, since the involvement of outside shareholders almost invariably has an impact on a company's policies and culture. As already mentioned, dealing effectively with the succession issue and making appropriate financing arrangements are the essential elements of ensuring continuity in the private sector. Every entrepreneur is personally responsible for these decisions, which are crucial to his company, his family, and his employees. It is his obligations to people and to society that are the key issue here—not the mere question of ownership.

To ensure the continuity of his company, an entrepreneur must make preparations from a very early stage with regard to determining how his company is to be run and financed after his death. These two aspects are closely linked to each other!

If he has children who are potentially capable of helping to run the business, then this solution must be put to the test as early as possible by training them and giving them responsibility for part of the company. If a solution along these lines has not taken credible shape by the time he reaches forty, then plans must be put in place to bring in someone from outside. Having the company managed by an outsider under the overall supervision of the family offers a perfectly appropriate way of ensuring continuity. In this event it is highly advisable to use the services of an experienced recruitment agency.

Advance planning to ensure continuity of financing is readily feasible and highly advantageous to the company in terms of securing its future. By involving any children in the company from an early date, the entrepreneur can greatly reduce the tax burden on his death. Their involvement can be arranged in such a way that no difficulties need arise as to who is in charge of what.

Enabling employees to have a share in the company's capital has, in my experience, proved very beneficial in respect to both financing and to increasing their identification with the company. It can also be very helpful to set up nonprofit-making trusts. In any event I should like to stress on the basis of my own experience that even today there is scope for ensuring the financial continuity of a company without resorting to the stock exchange. These alternative interpretations of "continuity" are very much in the interests of the entrepreneur, his family, and his employees!

Potentially calamitous contraventions of the maxim that the continuity of the state must always be safeguarded.

To further clarify the arguments set out above, I offer the following summary of things that pose a threat to the continuity of the state:

1. Rejection of transparency, competition, and modernization by politicians and the state sector in general;
2. failure to modernize the goals and systems of society;
3. incurring public debt at the expense of future generations;
4. curtailing freedom of opinion;
5. tolerating unnecessary monopolies;
6. failure to take all necessary steps to train the leaders of tomorrow, and failure to develop better management techniques;
7. refusal to undertake strategic planning;
8. neglecting to inculcate any clear ethical perspective;
9. handing out seats to politicians without prior proof of their competence;
10. accepting the notion that owning a business is sufficient qualification for running it.

LIMITATIONS OF THE HUMAN CAPACITY FOR CHANGE

When things are going badly, people hope for change. But in entertaining this very understandable hope, they fail to appreciate that change also means that they must alter their habits and learn to behave in new ways. This learning process is a real challenge, especially for older people.

People don't always believe in the possibility of change. If they lose all hope of a truly humane future, they often decide to emigrate. The hope of having a better life somewhere else is also kindled these days by the sometimes deceptively dreamy impression of other countries conveyed by television. But in the past, too, the discrepancy between people's hopeless plight in their own country and the seductive promise of distant lands has triggered numerous great waves of migration, and only rarely have the emigrants had any idea of the travails and deprivations that awaited them. As this phenomenon is now threatening to recur on a global scale, it would be sensible to make the emigration process more transparent, and to work out some alternative ways of dealing with the problem. For in most cases the intolerable circumstances that make people decide to emigrate can be rectified if reforms are put in place expeditiously. By helping people to help themselves, international aid could often make it unnecessary for them to leave their own countries, and thus prevent disappointment and social instability.

The example of migration casts a particularly clear light on the opportunities and dangers of the current period of change. Adjusting to a new culture takes time and requires those involved to alter their habits radically. It is precisely in periods of accelerated change that this can lead to explosive situations. In the last couple of centuries we have seen such things happen again and again in Germany, and this should have taught us what people without hope are capable of. If on the other hand we can control the pace of change, we can successfully get people to adapt to it. Politicians generally underestimate the length of time that people need in order to become accustomed to the consequences of change. The habits of thought and behavior that people so laboriously acquire are a great help to them in their journey through life! One can only hope that global competition will leave us sufficient time to deal adequately with the process of restructuring society and accustoming ourselves to a new kind of culture.

10

ENSURING THAT THE STATE
CAN LEARN NEW THINGS

SYSTEMS ARE ONLY VALID FOR A LIMITED PERIOD!

If progress and stability really matter to a society, it has to have the ability to respond to change. What this means in political terms today is that we have to *want* progress and *accomplish* progress. Our politicians must therefore ensure both now and in the future that those attributes of society that are necessary for its continued existence are more vigorously cultivated. These attributes rest on convictions and habits that in many cases—such as our system of values—go back hundreds of years.

When traditional beliefs have had their day and need to be replaced by a new code of values, it is likely to take a long time to get this new code across to people if it does not have majority support and needs a lot of getting used to! This requires a fundamental readjustment of people's opinions and attitudes; but since this process takes longer for some than others, there is a risk that very tough battles will break out along the road to a new culture—battles that in a worst-case scenario could threaten the very fabric of society.

Countless people would be affected by this, and the question therefore arises whether such processes of change can be rendered manageable. The shift in the basic premises of life over the last two hundred years clearly demonstrates that it is in the interests of all citizens that cultural change be managed and controlled. In some important respects the makings of a new value system are already at hand and need only be tested and implemented. It should not be forgotten, however, that reforms must be introduced with the greatest possible care if citizens are not to find them too taxing.

Can we offer any useful suggestions? It might be helpful to ascertain which historical systems reacted to social problems in a particularly flexible way, and thus had a marked ability to evolve. This might afford us insights that also help us to find appropriate solutions for the challenges facing us today. It would seem advisable, furthermore, to steer clear of ideological disputes; instead we should take a liberal, pluralistic approach to the problems of society, and measure the results that emerge against the yardstick of humane values—though I have to admit that the scope for measuring human behavior and drawing the appropriate political conclusions has not so far been adequately grasped in Germany, especially not by those in the political arena, who still have the tendency to proclaim opinions without making any attempt to substantiate them. No wonder, then, that dialogue is difficult and often goes nowhere.

Thanks to my experience in the Bertelsmann Foundation I know that the new science of testing and evaluation can yield results that could be successfully applied to politics. The only problem is that it is in so many people's interest to maintain the status quo that alternative systems are generally not given a moment's consideration—and if at all, then only when something has failed so completely that it can no longer be tolerated. And yet the experience of other areas of society has long since proved to the satisfaction of the relevant experts that transparency achieved through the introduction of measurability and comparability would be of real value in politics. There is a very simple yardstick that tells us whether an action is the right one, and therefore progressive, or the wrong one, and therefore doomed to failure, namely the yardstick of *competition* (albeit competition on a humane basis).

What we now need to do in all areas of society is to develop ways of doing things that lend themselves to evaluation and, as a result, carry complete conviction. In the course of hundreds of relevant projects undertaken by the Bertelsmann Foundation I have learned that it is possible to develop criteria for comparing and hence evaluating performance, and that in consequence these criteria represent a reliable and realistic assessment procedure that in conjunction with a probationary period enables risks to be minimized, and that also has the kind of credibility needed to influence public opinion. Our political leaders never tire of pointing out that the free market system with its crucial element of competition is the best possible arrangement, and one that lends itself to continual development. Why don't politicians draw the obvious conclusion that they should institute similar principles and practices within their own areas of responsibility? What is going on? Is it simply lack of knowledge? Or does the state still regard progress as a confounded nuisance?

TRANSPARENCY IN A DEMOCRACY

In Germany today opinion polls are regularly carried out by various private organizations, and one of the things that they reveal is the level of esteem in which the different professions are held by the public. It should give us considerable food for thought that politicians and trade unionists score worst of all—in other words, the very people who owe their positions of power to a democratic vote rather than to any proven ability. In the private sector, by contrast, it has long been realized that quality of management is the key factor in determining success, and that what matters here is not so much the methods used but the quality of the people using them. Applied to politics, this would mean that the decisive factor would have to be the *competence* of the candidate elected, and the methodology of the democratic election process would have to be a subordinate consideration. This has long been a familiar fact of life in other organizations geared to efficiency and success. I need only mention trade and industry, the armed forces, and academia! Organizations that are not success oriented, on the other hand, are prone to all sorts of manipulations and are correspondingly less well qualified.

One reason why too little account is taken of this state of affairs, however, is that totally inadequate attention is paid in politics to personnel matters and to the task of ensuring that potential leaders enter the profession. We thus have the extraordinary circumstance that lack of competition is preventing us from making progress that would otherwise be readily achievable.

This lamentable situation prompts the following observation: Voters can only make sound decisions about the alternatives offered to them in a democracy if they are given sufficient information about the individuals concerned, their goals, and their achievements. But despite the vast amounts of money and effort expended on election campaigns, the choices available to voters are insufficiently transparent to the great majority of them. In my opinion it is asking far too much of citizens to expect them to make considered decisions about candidates and parties in the current cacophony of political propaganda.

To see this problem in even sharper relief we need only look at the far greater perspicuousness of the decision-making process that determines the course of action to be taken by a corporation. Shareholders have to make important decisions affecting the company, but before doing so they are fully briefed, thanks to an auditing and informational process prescribed by law. Even though efforts have long been made throughout the entire world to render the decision-making process at shareholders' meetings fully effective, we still encounter numerous instances of wrong decisions. Thus it is plainly not easy even in the private sector to put large numbers of voters in the position where they can exercise their vote judiciously! And it is infinitely more difficult in the realm of politics where there is nowhere near the same level of auditing and information feedback that occurs in corporations, and where insufficient attention is paid to the need for transparency. To make our democracy function effectively, we should attempt—despite all the attendant difficulties—to establish criteria for all social developments, allowing us to see how they score in comparison with those in other countries, and thereby enabling us to make an informed assessment of policies and politicians. If an information system of this kind were to be prescribed by law, voters would have a much better basis on which to cast their vote! A scheme such as this that would modernize the democratic process is readily feasible, and there is no lack of the requisite money. What *is* lacking is the necessary will and willingness on the part of our legislators to enable voters to make proper assessments of politics and politicians! In public they constantly call for transparency in our democracy, but I believe that in truth they are afraid of its political consequences—and perhaps they also don't know how to bring it about.

In the meantime it remains difficult for voters to judge candidates nominated by the political parties. The media coverage that accompanies these nomination processes is sometimes helpful, but it is often misleading! Furthermore, recommendations of specific individuals are mostly rehashes of someone else's opinion and as such of questionable value! The position is somewhat different if one happens to see political candidates in person, either giving a speech or participating in a discussion. But these days there are very few opportunities to see first-rank politicians in person. Television is indeed helpful in this respect, but unfortunately it reveals only part of their personalities.

When democracy evolved in Greece thousands of years ago it was obviously much less of a problem to make judgments about people's personalities. In the far smaller cities of those days the speakers in the agora were all well known to the citizens. Everyone knew what to think about both them and their opinions. The risk of voters being deceived or facts manipulated was correspondingly low and offered practically no grounds for objection to the democratic system. We can't re-create the conditions in which people of that period formed their judgments about personalities—but the media could do far more than they do at present to give sound information as a basis for judgments about political candidates, and to make that information more comprehensible to voters. We need to recognize that the democratic imperative of transparency is indispensable to the proper functioning of our political system.

These principles of transparency and comprehensibility that are especially vital to a democracy are systematically and skillfully flouted today! Those responsible in the various parties need to realize that behavior of this kind diminishes democracy in a dangerous way! Promises of "jam tomorrow" go down well with the public—but such promises should not be made when there is neither the skill nor the money to deliver them! As the old adage has it: No one believes a liar, even when he's telling the truth!

SHAPING PUBLIC OPINION ON POLITICAL ISSUES

The politics of a democracy should reflect the views of a majority of the electorate. This fundamental principle presupposes that the electorate are given proper information on current policies and future plans so that they can bring sound opinions to bear when it comes to voting. The parliamentary method of shaping public opinion through the cut and thrust of party politics and the debates routinely conducted in the media are both well suited to demonstrating the pros and cons of proposed new policies. It is thus all the more lamentable that the state's information systems are not more strongly oriented toward transparency, efficiency, and competition. For one result of this is that even politicians find it very difficult to figure out the likely consequences of proposed new policies. These conditions are not conducive to proper planning and control, and they have the particular defect that very little thought is given to alternative solutions. There is no need for this to be the case! In this day and age ample information could be made available regarding all the activities undertaken by the state, and it would accordingly be possible to require that all proposed political projects be subjected to benchmarking, for instance, by comparing them to similar projects abroad. A comparison of this kind would make it starkly apparent to our politicians that we ought to have such data readily available, but also that many solutions that we think we have to laboriously work out for ourselves have already been successfully implemented somewhere else in the world. In the private sector this kind of procedure is standard practice! Our politicians should get used to it as a matter of urgency!

People today commonly tend to explain this lamentable state of affairs by complaining that there is no money available even for major projects—but it should be borne in mind that comparisons of method and efficiency of the kind outlined above would result in massive savings for the state! What I have demonstrated here is a way for politicians to learn much more about things—and it can be made a reality at relatively little cost. The Bertelsmann Foundation has based its work on this approach for many, many years. By these means we very rapidly and very economically find answers that never even occur to the state—as its international ranking clearly proves. This approach involving the use of international data is one that the Foundation will carry on banging the drum for until our politicians finally get it into their heads that they themselves should be using these tools on a routine basis.

What also needs to be corrected, however, is the public sector's antiquated notion of what its goals should be. At present, the electorate is only told whether the government has kept within the budget or exceeded it. Annual reports of this kind were simple and well suited to their purpose in the old days when the one great goal was to do everything by the book, but today they are totally inadequate. It is not enough for the government to declare that it has stayed within budget: People nowadays need to be told what has actually been achieved and not achieved—and they need to be told this more than once each year! As in the private sector, results must be reported with minimum delay—say, every three months—so that abortive developments can be more rapidly identified and corrected.

II

AN ECONOMIC ORDER BASED ON IDENTIFICATION

ENTERPRISE CULTURE AS THE ANSWER TO THE NEW CONDITIONS PREVAILING IN SOCIETY

The change in social circumstances that occurred during the twentieth century makes it imperative that in the world of work, too, traditional aims and working methods be brought up-to-date. An economic structure that is hierarchical and based on ownership rights entails such heavy losses through industrial unrest nowadays that for the sake of our competitiveness we have to ask whether we can conceive of a system better suited to the challenges now facing us.

We need first to cast a quick glance at the major disruptive factors currently affecting the economy:

1. Hierarchical structures cannot cope with the sheer quantity and difficulty of management tasks today.

2. The state thinks it can ease the burden on its citizens by imposing more and more regulations and more and more taxes on trade and industry. This practice is counterproductive.

3. The obvious answer of deregulating the various areas of responsibility and limiting the state's expenditure often comes to nothing because of a false conception of democracy. The principle of subsidiarity is ignored out of sheer opportunism!

4. Insufficient account is taken of the different perceptions that people have of themselves today. Employees are no longer underlings. They seek self-fulfillment! Not least within their community.

5. The purely national economies of the past have no future in a global market. A new system must therefore be devised that obviates or minimizes those elements that are known to stand in the way of progress.

PROPOSITIONS CONCERNING THE GOALS ENVISIONED UNDER THE ENTERPRISE CULTURE SYSTEM

1. The paramount task of the private sector is to provide society with products and services.

2. The representatives of the various interest groups active in the economy must represent the interests of their members in such a way that the overriding interests of society are not undermined. They share responsibility for the success of their company!

3. The Executive Board, in conjunction with the Supervisory Board, should assume responsibility for coordinating the interests of the different group representatives. The latter must also be rep-

resented on the Supervisory Board. So long as ownership carries decision-making rights, the annual general meeting of shareholders has the final say on major issues.

4. Employers, unions, and professional associations must support the company's management. They help to develop viable systems when this is not being successfully achieved within the company itself. The state may lay down general conditions governing these things.

5. Managers are keen to prove themselves. For this they need an entrepreneurial environment and, above all, freedom of action. They want to be creative, and they want to be a match for the competition. In a company dedicated to enterprise culture their relationships with their fellow employees must be based on partnership. Their pay should be largely dependent on their performances.

6. Today's ordinary workers also don't want merely to earn their living: By identifying with their companies and shouldering responsibility they seek to make positive contributions, to make full use of their opportunities, and to feel that they are doing something truly meaningful. Employee profit-sharing schemes ensure fairness at the material level, at the same time increasing staff motivation and hence company productivity! The work of employees must no longer be driven by coercion and harsh discipline, but by motivation born of a strong sense of identification!

7. The aim of capital is to achieve a high return and to ensure that their investment is secure. The investors' powers of control must these days be maintained through the selection of suitable people to sit on the Executive Board and through due supervision thereof. Capital can contribute to productivity by making social investments in the company. When membership of the Supervisory

Board is being determined, managerial competence must be the key criterion, ahead of any rights deriving from ownership.

THE ESSENTIALS OF ENTERPRISE CULTURE

Within the private sector, the goals that enterprise culture aspires to mean that the following elements are necessary:

Equality of opportunity: Everyone in the company must have the opportunity to gain promotion in accordance with his ability.

Primacy of performance: Financial compensation is determined by the level of performance achieved. Efforts by staff to acquire extra skills and qualifications are to be encouraged.

Profit sharing: In the interests of fairness, staff must be given a share of the company's profits.

Security of employment: The company must develop strategies to ensure its own continuation. Laying off workers must be avoided if at all possible.

Delegation of responsibility: To ensure effective management and to improve competitiveness, as many responsibilities as possible should be delegated to lower levels. It is an essential prerequisite of this process that staff identify fully with the company.

Strategy for ensuring management competence: In this period where all markets are expanding, the company must invest, well in advance, in its next generation of managers. Those involved in this personnel task must ensure that trainees are predisposed to accept the principles of enterprise culture.

Social welfare benefits: The working atmosphere within a company is considerably improved if it provides strong employee benefits! In this respect the company should regard itself as forming part of a civil society.

Keeping staff informed: For staff to identify with the company, they need to be kept sufficiently in the picture by means of in-house bulletins and detailed personal briefings by managers; questionnaires should be used to make regular checks on the general mood within the company.

By way of summary it might be noted that both here and abroad the enterprise culture concept has quite rapidly won warm approval from all concerned. It gives companies involved in the worldwide competition between different economic systems the opportunity to achieve international preeminence. Enterprise culture combines an emphasis on efficiency with a firm commitment to humane principles, and through both its products and its working conditions contributes to the stability of society.

TOWARD THE NEW ENTERPRISE CULTURE

This book has repeatedly emphasized the extent to which our thoughts and actions are determined by habit. As a result of the rapid pace of change in recent decades people are now beginning to realize that numerous traditional ways of doing things need to be thoroughly updated. In seeking to introduce enterprise culture we should stress that our economic system needs to acquire a "humane dimension," and clearly identify the improvements that the system requires. Our arguments must concentrate on the following aspects of the need for reform:

1. In view of the way employees perceive themselves today, identification, motivation, and informed understanding are indispensable if they are to give their best.

2. The manner in which labor disputes are conducted is inimical to the spirit of "trust and cooperation," which is even prescribed in law, and creates an atmosphere in the workplace that is detrimental to hard work and efficiency.

3. The conflict culture advocated and practiced by the tariff partners makes it much more difficult to delegate responsibility— yet this is an indispensable part of management today.

THE IMPLEMENTATION OF ENTERPRISE CULTURE

If, in view of the shortcomings of our current economic system, we wish to implement changes to bring it up-to-date, we have to find a way of doing so that is in accord with our constitution, and that our citizens will view as being both appropriate and in their own interest. This process will impinge on the interests of various different groups: the interests of those who actually work in the economy, but also the interests of politicians, who must ponder how best to win over the groups affected and thus gain their support for reforms along enterprise culture lines. This can perhaps most readily be achieved by comparing our own results with those of other companies and national economies with which we are in competition. It is therefore necessary—in conjunction with universities and research institutes—to commission many more such comparative studies of all relevant data on an international scale.

Because of the way they presently operate, politicians are so overburdened with work that they will not easily be won over to a new system—but they *can* be won over to alternative ideas if they think it would get the voters on their side. This is exactly what is most likely to happen in the case of the enterprise culture system, which indeed is likely to find approval among managers and workers alike. After all, enterprise culture has its very basis in the motivation and sense of identification of those who work in the economy, and in consequence could easily attract the interest of politicians as well.

The representatives of capital, on the other hand, will probably come to like enterprise culture at a much later stage. But when the comparisons of different economic systems required under the enterprise culture system lead to significantly higher profitability, capital will be prepared in the interests of its own success to accept such compromises as may be necessary in the cooperative endeavors of the various interest groups.

The really cogent arguments in favor of reform on enterprise culture lines may therefore be summarized as follows:

1. Success will be the deciding factor!
2. The process can be accelerated by the use of appropriate comparisons with other economic systems.
3. Academic experts must be involved in verifying the assessment process.
4. The tariff partners must be included in the dialogue about enterprise culture.

Cultures take a long time to develop and grow. We can only hope that the pressures of international competition leave us enough time to test and implement the new enterprise culture system. The attempt is well worth making, as it is a system capable of tapping untold energies, for the simple reason that it is geared to human beings. This has been my own experience of enterprise culture in the course of my professional life. I can therefore well imagine that within a few years international rankings will show that an economy derives a crucial advantage from adopting the enterprise culture system. It is certain that it would improve the competitiveness of Germany.

12

THE FUTURE OF ENTERPRISE CULTURE

THE IMPORTANCE TO ENTERPRISE CULTURE OF A CLEAR SENSE OF VALUES

The history of mankind repeatedly demonstrates that in order to regulate their community human beings both need and welcome rules in the form of ethical imperatives and binding laws. The principles governing good order in a society are determined by the prevailing circumstances of people's lives and by the way in which they perceive themselves. These factors make allowance for the immutable attributes of human nature; at the same time, however, they are influenced by developments within the culture— and so in this sense they are flexible and capable of being interpreted in different ways.

We have to decide what foundations our society can be built on, and what goals it should set for itself. The way we perceive ourselves today is a far cry from the mentality of the serf-like subjects of old who put up with their autocratic rulers more or less out of conviction. Today we have to build our world according to a very different conception of man! Europe and the European conception of man have been shaped principally by Christian doctrine, Greek philosophy, and Roman law. From these roots grew both our respect for human life, and our desire to fashion our lives as we ourselves see fit. Barriers of geography and language led to the evolution of many special features in different localities, but the conception of man underlying the social and legal systems of the various nations reflected the values of the Western world.

In the course of the twentieth century, however, the importance of national boundaries was greatly relativized by developments in trade and communications, and what we are now seeing is a reduction of the rights and powers of nation-states. But the structures of the European Union that are presently taking shape will nonetheless—despite all the special features of different regions—still reflect the values of the Western world and the shared conception of man that they gave rise to. In effect, the most important driving forces behind the whole modernization process derive from aspirations and assumptions already inherent in our culture. By way of example I would refer readers to the vast restructuring of entire societies that took place in the twentieth century as a result of the demand for more justice and more solidarity!

The leaders of any society will succeed and endure only if they know how to reconcile the demands of the individual with the rights of his fellow citizens. Furthermore, the ability to live in a community is something that has to be taught, and then refined through practice. Everyone must realize that they cannot expect only to *take* from society; they also have an obligation to *give* to society!

In the second half of the twentieth century the government of the Federal Republic had to devote much effort to shaping the relationship between the citizen and the democratic state of which he was part. Setting new goals—both for the individual and for society as a whole—was one aspect of this. The state itself, with the vast array of services that it provides, has had to learn that its traditional goal of always sticking to the rules is no longer sufficient in these times.

The political debates of the last few decades not only highlighted the ongoing reappraisal of the conception of man, they also taught us that consensus can only be achieved in the political and economic realms if there is at least minimal agreement regarding the values that give our culture its particular stamp. In the twentieth century the conflict culture approach was intensively used, and indeed achieved considerable results; today, however, we find that it is extremely difficult to make constructive progress unless there is a sufficient basis of agreement about fundamental ethical questions. It should be plain enough to us from our history books that the restructuring of a society takes a long time. I am therefore confident that we will accomplish the change, provided that we are sufficiently patient, purposeful, and willing to shoulder responsibility!

With regard to the process of democratization, it did not take people in Europe very long to realize that they could reasonably expect a high level of services and benefits from the state, and enjoy a greater degree of personal freedom; but they have still not sufficiently understood the rules of the game in a democracy, which require *them* to make an equivalent contribution in return. Only very slowly are a few individuals beginning to volunteer to take on social responsibilities—and in so doing they are beginning to grasp the principle of subsidiarity. This learning process should be reinforced by our politicians!

The ethical and political reorientation process that is already under way has to be carried through by politicians and citizens alike. Parents must once again start teaching their children how to become good citizens. The education system must then build on these beginnings and train its charges in readiness for their role as independent and responsible members of society. In this, we should also bear in mind that freedom comes not at the beginning of the learning process but at its end, as a reward for having mastered the art of being a responsible member of society. All those responsible for educating the young must always remember that they can achieve a great deal in our society simply by setting a good example.

Religious institutions have always played an especially important role in education. History shows that by virtue of their particular structure and mission the various churches simply had no equal in the way they managed to instill values—and make those values stick. But reviving old belief systems will not get us very far in our efforts to reestablish a clear sense of values; people's perceptions of themselves and the circumstances of their existence have changed too much for that to be possible. Instead, calm reflection, a clear perspective, and a willingness to learn are the order of the day. With regard to the reformative work that needs to be done, it seems to me likely that the task of re-creating a clear sense of values will be undertaken by smaller groups fired by commitment and conviction—and that they will do a better job than large organizations with set doctrines.

As management techniques have evolved it has become very clear to me how hard it is for large organizations—be it in trade and industry or the public sector, in the armed forces or the church—when they have to undergo major reforms. In the church this is made all the more difficult by their body of doctrine. But in view of today's lack of any clear ethical perspective, so dangerous both for the individual and for society as a whole, I must call on the churches to take a long, hard look at themselves. Is their message one that people today still want to hear, and are they giving them answers to their questions? I myself am convinced that a sense of values that conveys both belief and motivation is just as indispensable to human beings as education and an adequate standard of living.

The factors that decisively influence our thinking and culture today are very different from those that prevailed in the nineteenth century with its distinctly conservative and religious slant.

The family in those days fulfilled numerous protective functions for which the state has now assumed responsibility. The world of work did not have anything like the significance it has now, particularly for women. This whole world with its far narrower range of experiences was characterized by severe constraints and strict hierarchical systems. Viewed from our vantage point today, the social structures of the time allowed little opportunity for self-fulfillment. However, we should be careful not to disparage this as a "backward" culture, for it matched the realities of the time.

As for the citizens of today, a whole variety of influences have made them open to the idea of their culture being brought up-to-date, especially their higher standard of living, their greater freedom, and the security afforded them by social welfare legislation. In this context we should also not forget the dominant influence of that twentieth-century phenomenon, the mass media! In the now very important world of work, efforts are under way to develop systems based on the spirit of partnership, with motivation and identification taking the place of compulsion. The global market and the pressures of competition are forcing us to move forward in this way, and this in turn creates a need for more people who are creative and independent minded. Strict discipline can no longer be the sole driving force behind employees such as these! Anyone bearing any kind of responsibility today must be motivated by delight at having the opportunity to be creative and to realize their potential, and must be convinced that the goals and successes of their company benefit not only them but society as a whole. A stance of this sort is indispensable to the management techniques of devolved responsibility, and as such accords well with the requirements of competitiveness.

In a company that is based on a spirit of partnership and run along entrepreneurial lines, the attitude of senior staff is observed and discussed by countless people every day. Any standard of behavior that a manager demands of his subordinates must equally apply to himself. There have been frequent instances in my experience where senior staff—for whatever reason—have been untruthful or have availed themselves on the sly of improper perks. Aberrations of this sort undermine employees' trust in and respect for the manager concerned and make it more difficult for them to identify with the company. Damaging habits then proliferate at all levels like a plague. Employees expect absolute probity in their superiors! The goals of the entrepreneur must be geared to people and to society. And this stance should be manifest not only in his professional life but also in his life within his community. For people quite rightly expect everyone in a democracy to shoulder civic duties to the full extent of their capabilities! Alongside his professional work, therefore, the entrepreneur should play an active part in civil society.

A clear sense of values will undoubtedly help people to find their places in society and adopt the right attitudes toward their fellow human beings. Each and every one of us is in some way dependent on the help of our community. The success, not to mention the happiness, of individuals thus depends to a very considerable extent on their building their relationship with society in the right way. Thus when it comes to evaluating their potential goals, people's priorities change in keeping with the realities of the age and their own self-perceptions. Given our particular history in the twentieth century, we should also remember that it is extremely risky to pursue false goals or to try to live in a community without the help of a clear set of values. A society can only endure if it is also possessed of a culture of shared values!

WHAT ARE THE PROSPECTS FOR ENTERPRISE CULTURE?

I know full well that many entrepreneurs do not yet share my view of the potential benefits of the enterprise culture system, and that most people on the employers' side accept the customary method of arriving at decisions by hammering things out with the unions in conflict culture mode. I must also admit that at the start of my career many other entrepreneurs warned me against making innovations. It is very clear to me that for the time being at least it would be premature to introduce enterprise culture on a universal basis.

It is nevertheless my firm conviction that cooperation between the different interest groups can be extremely successful, and could be distinctly superior to conflict culture as regards international competition. The decision as to what constitutes the right system for our economy does not have to be made today. Instead we should look at the enterprise culture system with an objective eye and try it out! Again and again in this book I have drawn attention to the fact that changed circumstances in the private sector call for new goals and new directions. Does the enterprise culture system have a future? We should wait and see whether this new concept proves successful in practice. But even today there are many entrepreneurs and managers who go along with the Bertelsmann model and apply it in their companies, while the unions also view it with critical interest, though they doubtless do not consider our particular solution to be generally applicable, or at any rate not at the present time. But I well remember President John F. Kennedy at the Berlin Wall prophesying to the socialist countries that freedom could prove infectious. This may one day turn out to be true of enterprise culture, too.

I can live with criticism and counterarguments! After all, I myself am keen to emphasize that enterprise culture has yet to prove its worth, and that only time will tell whether this system with its combination of cooperativeness, humanity, dedication, and self-fulfillment really is superior to any other. But this is precisely what I have been trying to prove throughout my professional career, and certainly the enterprise culture we introduced at Bertelsmann has turned out to be extremely successful. It is surely beyond question that Germany must tread new paths and have the courage to implement reforms, and in this respect enterprise culture seems to me to offer a very promising example of what can be done. It doesn't impede Bertelsmann's ongoing dialogue with politicians and with employers and unions. We are self-critical and willing to learn, but we are also set on success! And we have the courage to try new ways of doing things, and we are accordingly putting our money on the enterprise culture system!

IMPLEMENTING THE GOAL OF ENTERPRISE CULTURE

The Bertelsmann Administrative Company (Bertelsmann Verwaltungsgesellschaft mbh, or "BVG") is required to exercise its voting rights at General Meetings of the Bertelsmann Corporation (Bertelsmann AG) in line with the Bertelsmann Corporation's goals and enterprise culture.

There are eight shareholders in all: five management staff nominated by the company, and three other members chosen by the Mohn family.

The Task of the BVG

Developments in economic systems

Over the past two centuries the various economic systems in use around the world have undergone profound changes. Imaginative and successful entrepreneurs set an example by trying out new ways of doing things. We are all well aware that as a result of international competition everything is now subject to constant and fundamental change, from the goals that a company sets itself right through to its internal organization.

Germany over the past two centuries saw the development of an economic system that aimed to achieve social justice and give maximum consideration to human beings and their needs, and to this end adopted a procedure derived from democratic politics whereby disagreements are resolved by the parties simply battling it out, with strikes as the ultimate weapon. For a long period of time progress was indeed achieved by these means. Today, however, given the new way in which people perceive themselves, this method of decision making no longer works. Unemployment and lack of competitiveness are clear symptoms of this.

After the Second World War the Bertelsmann company followed its own chosen path, rethinking both its goals and its whole way of working. This path proved highly successful, and is supported by all the various interest groups involved in the company. The concept took shape in the phenomenon known as the "Bertelsmann enterprise culture."

Redefining our goals

The biggest single change in our system concerned the company's goals as perceived by management and staff. Instead of following the usual procedure and rating the company's performance solely according to profit and growth, we measured it in terms of the contribution it made to society at the human level. Profit and growth are not so much goals in themselves, but rather a yardstick for gauging the success of the company's activities and the rightness of one's own course of action. In addition, profits are an essential prerequisite of the second most important goal, that of ensuring continuity—in other words, ensuring that the company remains adaptable and capable of developing in new directions in the future. This change of goals proved to be the right move, and it became the crucial basis for our subsequent success.

The innovative elements in our approach are as follows:

- profit sharing as a financing tool and as an important contribution to economic fairness;
- particular emphasis on the company's social responsibilities;
- conducting all relationships within the company in a spirit of partnership;

- and, above all, a new conception of the interaction between management and capital.

In our organization a different kind of status is accorded to the rights of control conferred by ownership. Given the history of the Industrial Revolution and especially of the rise of the entrepreneur, we are very well aware that the success of a business is chiefly determined by the skill of those who manage it and give it its specific shape and direction. In medium-size companies this is still impressively evident in the person of owner-entrepreneurs. In large companies, on the other hand, management techniques are fundamentally different today, for it is no longer possible to run things on a hierarchical and centralistic basis; there has to be specialization of managerial responsibilities, and there has to be delegation! To this end, the company's employees have to be convinced that its goals are right and that a cooperative response would be to their advantage. At the same time the company's managers have to learn to perceive their roles in a new way! They can no longer lead simply by virtue of the authority vested in them. Delegation of responsibility is indispensable—but it can only be done if all concerned identify with the company's goals and the new conception of how it is to be run.

In talking about "running" the company, however, we must not think only of the man at the very top, but also of the numerous managers who have taken on decentralized responsibilities. This applies equally to line managers and to managers with specific responsibilities in company administration and on executive committees. It is my experience that the managers who are fully aware of their responsibilities and associated decision-making powers exercise these powers in a highly motivated way, develop a particularly creative approach to their work, and thus make a significant contribution to the company's success.

This latter remark is also true of those elected by their fellow employees as members of the Works Committee. As a result of their influence there is a better understanding of decisions, and management is made aware of any action that needs to be taken, all of which helps to improve motivation and reduce friction and the losses that it causes. It is therefore only logical that three staff representatives and one management representative sit on the Supervisory Board of Bertelsmann AG while the BVG shareholders' group includes a member of the Works Committee, the Chairman of the Board of Bertelsmann AG, plus one further member of the company's management team.

Our business concept and the task of the BVG

Our business system and management concept, having proved their worth so spectacularly within the space of only a few decades, needed to be institutionally anchored to ensure that our "enterprise culture" is fully implemented and further refined. We have entrusted this task to the BVG (Bertelsmann Verwaltungsgesellschaft). The BVG's statutes lay down that implementation of "enterprise culture" is to be its key task, alongside the other tasks it already carries out. This ensures that the goals arising from the principles defined in our enterprise culture are understood and heeded, and in due course updated.

Since 1999 it has been the BVG that determines how the voting rights of the Foundation and the family are to be exercised at the General Meeting—rights that were previously in the hands of Reinhard Mohn alone. This relates to decisions on the following matters: increases in capital; other changes in statutes; appointment of members of the Supervisory Board; appointment of auditors; use of balance-sheet profit; approving the actions of members of the Executive Board and the Supervisory Board. In addition, the BVG decides on recommendations for the appointment or removal of chairmen of the Executive Board and Supervisory Board. The distribution of responsibilities as between the Executive Board, the Supervisory Board, and the General Meeting is no different from that of other large corporations in Germany.

Following my departure, three of the eight BVG shareholders are provided by the Mohn family. The other five shareholders are all essentially managerial (Chairman of the Supervisory Board; a further member of the Supervisory Board; Chairman of the Executive Board; a staff representative; and one other member recruited from the Executive Board, from the management of a Bertelsmann holding company, or from the Bertelsmann Foundation's Board of Trustees); these five constitute the majority at shareholders' meetings, the decisions of which are arrived at by majority vote. The BVG has no operational responsibilities.

In certain rare cases the "simple majority" rule does not apply, namely when there is any possibility that a resolution of the BVG or of the Bertelsmann Corporation's General Meeting could alter the company's definition of its goals. In such cases a majority of three quarters of the votes is required for a motion to be approved. If the Mohn family's representatives vote against a motion requiring this three-quarters majority, then the requisite majority cannot be achieved. This means that the General Meeting of the Bertelsmann Corporation cannot make certain decisions—such as an increase in capital or a change in the statutes—without the approval of the Mohn family. It should be pointed out in this context that the family likewise cannot succeed with any motions affecting the company without the support of other shareholders—and in any event that is not its role as laid down in the statutes of the BVG.

RECOMMENDATIONS CONCERNING THE INTRODUCTION OF ENTERPRISE CULTURE

A social system with its many and diverse areas of responsibility can only be developed gradually and over a long period of time. People will learn new things—but they will probably make progress more through force of circumstance than through their own free choice. The private sector is the best place to start the reforms, given the strong competitive pressures that bear on it. No new political or legal decisions are required. Businesses are free to opt for the enterprise culture system, and the methodology is both well known and well tried. The advantages of a management method based on identification and motivation seem to me to be incontrovertible. Within a few years enterprise culture will have become more widely adopted and accepted within the private sector—and it will then be easier for politicians to apply the system in the public sector as well. Thus, for instance, it is perfectly possible to evaluate outcomes in the public sector by applying relevant criteria; this produces competition, from which certain conclusions can readily be drawn. I hope and expect that on the basis of the experience we have already gained at the Bertelsmann Foundation, a number of municipalities and state service-providers will soon seek to introduce competition and make efficiency a prime objective. I am thinking particularly of the administrative function in town halls, hospitals, schools, and libraries. Local initiatives of this sort can be carried out with little difficulty. Given the higher levels of efficiency, flexibility, and acceptance that they produce, they could greatly facilitate the extension of the system to the entire state sector.

Our political system will probably submit itself to such reforms last of all. The realm of politics has very clearly not been subject to sufficiently intense modernizing pressures. It is to be hoped, however, that the successes of enterprise culture in other areas of the state will at some point in the future have a positive effect on our politicians' working methods! While acknowledging that the reforms that enterprise culture makes possible would take a long time to achieve, be it in the economy, in the public sector, or in politics, we should also point out that these reforms would not only breathe new life into our systems right across the board, but would make them capable of learning new things!

The potential benefits of the enterprise culture system could be summed up as follows:

1. In the private sector, the strong sense of identification and the cooperative spirit shared by everyone involved results in greater success, increased professional opportunities, greater fairness, and higher levels of satisfaction. In consequence, the competitiveness of our country would be improved.

2. Within the apparatus of the state, enterprise culture produces competition, transparency, scope for individual initiative, and a strong focus on efficiency. It greatly enhances employee motivation, ensures rapid progress, and brings large cost savings.

3. In politics our system of democracy must be totally restructured. To this end it will be necessary to set up a "Systems Development Institute" to ensure that our system is capable of learning new methods. In this context I should stress that it is our political order that most urgently needs reforming!

13

EXAMPLES OF THE WORK OF THE BERTELSMANN FOUNDATION

O ver the last twenty-five years the Bertelsmann Foundation has proved that the state's services are just as amenable as anything else to being made both efficient and competitive. Some examples are listed below.

EDUCATION

Example I: Ranking of Universities

Competition exists in the German university system only in rudimentary form; there is no genuine competition for the best students. Competition for resources is still in its infancy, and as a rule is limited to one federal state. It is solely in respect to research funding that the universities are in real competition with one another. For decades it was policy in Germany to foster the myth that all German universities were equally good. Performance comparisons were regarded as inappropriate.

The ranking of universities that has been carried out for five years now by the Center for University Development in conjunction with *Stern* magazine seeks to make the German university system transparent in order to help prospective students to make the right choices. This overview thus doubles as an assessment and a recommendation.

Results of the project

Ranking not only makes people aware of differences in quality, but also engenders competition. It enables each university to compare itself to others.

• Many faculties use the rankings as a starting point for an analysis of their strengths and weaknesses, and this feeds into their efforts to reform their study programs. As a result there is an increasing demand for detailed analysis and evaluation of performance.

• Those responsible for the quality of teaching and learning within the various faculties (deans of study, for instance) are particularly likely to use *negative* outcomes in the ranking exercise to strengthen the case for reform, and to make their faculties pay more attention to teaching.

• Many universities who do well in the rankings make a special point of using this fact as an advertising and marketing tool. Typical examples of this are the University of Paderborn and Nordakademie, the privately funded economics college.

In a considerable number of cases the rankings have helped to focus attention on deficiencies within a particular faculty. In some instances specific changes can be directly attributed to the ranking exercise; at the Free University of Berlin, for example, the ranking outcomes led to goals jointly determined by the central authorities and the faculties that were specifically designed to eradicate deficiencies.

The ranking outcomes are also used by a growing number of students in choosing a university:

• Approximately one third of all students take the rankings into account when choosing a university. Overall it is clear that achievement-oriented applicants are the group that chiefly use the rankings.

• Ranking has a demonstrable effect on the numbers applying to individual universities.

Last but not least, the ranking system now receives extensive coverage in the press. The regional media in particular give detailed reports on how their local universities have fared. This puts intense pressure on universities with poor results to justify their existence—pressure they cannot ignore. By the same token, universities are practically forced to take part in these data collection exercises if they don't want to run the risk of simply not appearing in the rankings at all.

Example 2: Index of Libraries

Libraries are subject to a variety of pressures—from the public bodies that fund them, from the information needs of their customers, and from developments in the different media. Particularly against the background of difficult financial constraints it is important to make the requisite process of change an efficient one.

In 1999 the BIX Index of Libraries was created in order to improve the efficiency of libraries, and to provide decision makers in the libraries themselves, in their parent bodies, and in politics with a sound basis for agreeing on goals. At the time of this writing two hundred libraries are involved. In June 2002 the project was extended for another three years, and in this second phase university libraries will also be included.

The annual results are published in the BIX magazine and on the project's home page in the form of multidimensional rankings.

Results of the project

When the results are published each year in the summer, their effects are plain to see on a variety of levels.

• The process of evaluation and goal-setting undertaken by the library, the parent body, and the relevant political authorities is put on a sound footing by means of performance indicators and comparisons between different municipalities. The BIX Index provides a basis for agreeing on the parent body's commitment in terms of resource-provision over the coming financial year, and the library's commitment in terms of performance vis-à-vis its customers.

• Within the libraries themselves the comparative data are used as a basis for reviewing their performance and range of services, and for initiating optimization processes. There is a broad-based discussion of how to improve efficiency, enhance the library's profile, and develop appropriate goals and strategies.

• The local press takes much more interest in its local libraries. The stimulus for this is normally the publication of the rankings, which then triggers a public discussion of library services, costs, and the responsibilities of politicians and administrators. This occurs regardless of a library's position in the rankings.

Already in 2001, the BIX Index results led to specific optimization measures being instigated at approximately 30 percent of participating libraries. Measures introduced by the libraries themselves are aimed at enhancing efficiency by either streamlining their procedures or altering their collections policy. At the municipal level, the BIX results were taken into account when agreeing on goals, planning library developments, and managing contracts.

Example 3: International Network of Innovative School Systems (INIS)

In this network teachers, experts in administration, academics, and politicians involved in education exchange experience and pursue the transfer of knowledge between different school systems. Begun in 2001, the project concentrates on enhancing the quality of schools on the basis of international comparisons.

At present the project involves thirty-seven schools from Germany (Thuringia, Lower Saxony, North Rhine-Westphalia, Hessen), Canada, New Zealand, Holland, Norway, Scotland, Switzerland, and Hungary.

The aim of the project is to arrive at a shared perception of quality and then to promote it by comparing quality on an international basis. This is intended to enable schools to plan and evaluate their development processes more effectively and efficiently.

Results of the project

The first data-collecting exercise took place in April 2002; views on the effects of the exercise and the measures resulting from it were exchanged at the annual INIS conference in September 2002. A number of concrete outcomes have already been achieved, as follows:

- An internationally agreed-upon set of criteria for a good school;
- evaluative tools for surveying the opinions of parents, students, and teachers;
- document analysis of existing informational literature;
- introduction of a management information system;
- drawing up of action plans by participating schools on the basis of the relevant quality measurements.

The Bertelsmann Foundation has guaranteed the schools that for the time being it will not publish any of the data collected under the project.

DEMOCRACY AND CIVIL SOCIETY

Example I: Enhancement of Performance Comparisons for Municipalities

Using the classic benchmarking model, municipalities compared themselves with others on the basis of product-oriented indicators focusing on mission accomplishment, customer satisfaction, staff satisfaction, and value for money; analysis of the collected data then told them what improvements they needed to make. As a result, municipalities developed a better appreciation of what it means to be performance oriented, and qualitative improvements were soon introduced in abundance.

Key indicators in municipalities (KiK)

The KiK project was begun in 2000 and, just like classic benchmarking, works with the same four principal areas of focus mentioned above—but significantly reduces the amount of quantification required from those submitting data. In conjunction with experts experienced in municipal affairs, sets of indicators—numerically few but operationally crucial—have already been developed for the following areas: social welfare, youth welfare, personnel, economic development, and matters of public order (registration of residents, identity cards, trading standards, etc.). Sets of indicators are currently also being developed for the following areas of responsibility: management of traffic and green spaces, building control, finance, and schools and arts administration; as a result, it will soon be possible to produce profiles of all relevant areas of a municipality's administrative work.

The reports are generated by means of a data bank linked to the Internet, with the result that data is very easily collected. Comparisons based on indicators are currently being used by some forty municipalities; approximately eighty others have expressed interest in joining the scheme.

Results of the project
- Thanks to its quality assurance program conducted within the context of the KiK performance comparison, the town of Coesfeld has extended the hours of its Citizens' Office and has developed fully integrated work procedures.
- Also in Coesfeld, residents are now sent individual reminders when their identity cards are about to expire. This has resulted in a more even flow of visitors to the relevant office, and even greater customer satisfaction.
- The processing period for planning applications has also been reduced on average by 50 percent.
- In addition to the above-mentioned outcomes, the town of Herford has achieved great improvements in cooperation between the Citizens' Office, the Registry Office, and the Finance Office. As a result, people have to see fewer officials, business is transacted more rapidly, and resources are freed up.
- The town of Gütersloh has specified minimum sizes for children's playgrounds. As a result, quality has been enhanced and maintenance costs reduced.

Example 2: Model Municipalities

How good is the quality of life in German towns and cities? How do they react to social problems? What are the effects of demographic change? What do municipalities do to encourage employment and attract new companies to their area? These questions are at the heart of the Model Municipalities project that the Bertelsmann Foundation, together with nine German municipalities, has been working on since the year 2000.

The main aim of this project is to improve the effectiveness of municipal control mechanisms. To this end a control system has been developed that enables the political leadership of a municipality to rapidly identify and deal with weak areas and potential problems in town, county, or parish.

The project is based on the following key elements:

- Developing an information system so that quality of life can be measured *in situ*;
- making things transparent for local citizens, and publishing the relevant data in the form of benchmarks for the various municipalities involved;
- working out long-term political goals with local councilmen (i.e., elected municipal representatives) in conjunction with local citizens;
- deciding what concrete measures are necessary to ensure that towns develop in ways that are fully open to the future.

The participating municipalities are currently analyzing the data collected by the project, and on this basis adjusting their priorities within the context of budgetary planning. Given the present financial position of the municipalities, this represents an important management and control tool for local representatives and officials, while also creating transparency for voters with regard to the way scarce resources are being used.

Results of the project

Special attention is being focused on the following key areas:

- Managing democratic change: creating infrastructures suited to the elderly, monitoring the housing needs and quality of life of the elderly, supporting families;
- supporting children and young people, especially the socially disadvantaged;
- social cohesion and integration of foreigners.

There is great interest in this project at the municipal level. We began with six municipalities, three more joined in 2001 after the initial trial phase, and twenty others have expressed an interest in taking part.

Example 3: Lively Schools in Lively Towns

In this project, begun in 1998, the performance comparisons in respect to various municipalities were further developed into a strategic tool for use in the formulation of municipal policy. The specific aims of the project are as follows:

- To confirm the status of education as an area requiring strategic action;
- to create transparency by publishing reports on education within a given municipality;
- to draw up and implement action plans geared to specific needs;
- to strengthen education networks in towns participating in the project.

In conjunction with politicians, town hall officials, members of the public, and school representatives, appropriate goals and measurement categories were agreed upon for the municipal education sector—the first time that such a thing has happened in Germany. The resulting information-feedback system provides comprehensive data, for instance on educational opportunities, counseling arrangements, pastoral care—or even on the provision of up-to-date IT equipment in schools. All data collected under the auspices of the project are publicly discussed and are used as the basis for determining political priorities. The information is updated annually.

Results of the project

Following publication of the data in the spring of 2000, two important action areas have crystallized:

- The need to assist educationally disadvantaged children from immigrant families;
- the need to help students make the transition from school to employment.

The new information-feedback system brought these problems very clearly to light. In Arnsberg, for example, 20 percent of foreign students did not graduate from high school. The proportion of foreign children at special-needs schools was more than 40 percent in some towns, whereas the proportion at high schools was well below 3 percent. An opinion poll of parents and students revealed a high level of dissatisfaction in all towns over the lack of support for young people moving from school to employment. For example, only some 30 percent of those polled were satisfied with existing career counseling. The six towns involved in the project (Arnsberg, Castrop-Rauxel, Herford, Herten, Minden, and Unna) have reacted to these challenges with action plans that were then built into the municipal budget.

An interim evaluation of the project was undertaken in December 2002. A survey of target groups revealed particularly positive results in Arnsberg and Herten, where respondents rated the efforts of both towns as "good" (the second-highest rating on a five-point scale from "inadequate" to "very good"). All the towns involved in the pilot phase of the project are continuing their various initiatives independent of the support provided by the Bertelsmann Foundation. Münster and Mannheim are among the towns that have agreed to serve as knowledge-transfer centers.

HEALTH

Example: Center for Hospital Management

The Kerckhoff Hospital in Bad Nauheim incurred clear losses in 1992 that threatened its existence despite its good reputation in purely medical terms. Its management system was cameralistic and centralistic; its employees were paid on the federal salary scale for public servants.

Its management was then changed from a public-sector-type structure to one geared specifically to the needs and interests of staff and patients. This was coupled with an incentive scheme offering rewards to staff for making suggestions for improvements, willingness to undertake further training, passing on the benefits of further training, etc. Both staff representatives and middle management were involved in distributing the funds available under this incentive scheme.

The hospital has since won the Golden Helix Award, Europe's most notable prize for quality management in the health sector. Over a period of ten years, efficiency was increased by almost 70 percent, with almost the same number of staff, by using all the benefits of rationalization and by optimizing administrative procedures and the functionality of buildings and facilities. A hotel section was integrated into the site as early as 1996 to accommodate relatives and outpatients from outlying areas. In its capacity as a model hospital the Kerckhoff has led the way with its many pioneering initiatives—for instance, by introducing certified guarantees for certain medical procedures.

Profits have been such as to enable the construction of new buildings and the extension of others, together with other projects such as a rooftop landing pad for rescue helicopters and a state-of-the-art intensive care unit.

14

CONCLUSION:
A HUMANE ALTERNATIVE

This book analyzes the reasons for society's failure to meet the challenge of the age, and on the basis of this analysis shows what needs to be done to bring about a more humane order of things in the economic arena and in society as a whole. Human nature is characterized both by communal and by selfish impulses. The course of human history right up to the present day still gives us no clear indication as to which of these basic human tendencies will ultimately prevail. What is absolutely clear, however, is that only the aspiration to be part of a community combined with a determination to follow one's own individual path through life has produced progress and stability. We all realize that the challenges of the future are very soon going to necessitate fundamental reform, particularly in Germany; I shall therefore summarize and clarify the arguments put forward in this book by offering the following set of propositions:

PROPOSITION I

Our society needs a system of values that ensures peace and a strong sense of community.

PROPOSITION 2

By updating our concept of democracy to embrace transparency, fairness, humane values, and efficiency, we can expect to make real progress while also ensuring continuity.

PROPOSITION 3

Our systems must no longer be focused on size, maximum profit, or power. Instead we must have a new system that aims for ethical values, integration into the community, and social progress. To this end it must insist on the full involvement of all citizens, and must place them under an obligation to make their own contribution in accordance with the principle of subsidiarity. Solidarity and subsidiarity must counterbalance each other!

PROPOSITION 4

The leaders of this new social system must not rely on hierarchical structures. On the contrary, its effectiveness will derive from the successful application of the principle of delegated responsibility, from transparency, and from motivation. To this end it will utilize the productive forces of competition and performance-orientation everywhere.

PROPOSITION 5

The key criterion for judging whether the aims and methods of such a system are correct will be the fairness and humanity of its effects on society.

PROPOSITION 6

A culture geared to humane values has the ability to release enormous energies by activating people's powers of motivation and identification.

PROPOSITION 7

To safeguard a social order of this kind it is necessary to review it constantly and to make appropriate adjustments if and when people's self-perception changes.

PROPOSITION 8

I am grateful for the fact that within my own particular area of responsibility I was able to see the unexpected strengths that can reveal themselves in people once they identify with their community. My advice is that *this* is the path we should follow in order to create a new social order.

INDEX

ABOUT THE AUTHOR

REINHARD MOHN has served as chairman of both the Executive Board and the Supervisory Board of Bertelsmann, one of the largest media companies in the world. His fifty-plus years of service to the company began after World War II. Mohn wanted to pursue a career in engineering, but his father persuaded him to take over the family printing and publishing business. Mohn was soon managing the company, and over the years he transformed what had been a small family business into an international media powerhouse.

Mohn has received several awards throughout his illustrious career, among them the Order of Merit with Star of the Federal Republic of Germany; the European Philanthropic Prize; the Schumpeter Prize; the Hanns Martin Schleyer Award; the Fugger Medal; and the highly regarded Príncipe de Asturias Prize. He is also the author of *Success Through Partnership: An Entrepreneurial Strategy* (Doubleday, 1996) and *Humanity Wins* (Crown, 2000).